Victoria Crosses
of the Anglo-Boer War

Victoria Crosses
of the
Anglo-Boer War

Ian Uys

FORTRESS
Established 1973

Published by Fortress Financial Group (Pty) Ltd
P O Box 2475
Knysna 6570
South Africa

ISBN 0-620-25447-5

© Ian Uys 2000
First published 2000

Printed by: Knysna Press, P.O. Box 118, Knysna, 6570, South Africa

Acknowledgements

I am grateful for assistance received through the years from the South African National Museum of Military History in Johannesburg, the Imperial War Museum and the National Army Museum in London. My late friend, Canon Lummis MC had his research papers deposited at the latter in Chelsea. I appreciate the Military Historical Society allowing me access to these files. Thanks are also due to the publishers of the various reference works from which I have quoted and for the use of photographs.

I am especially grateful to Natalie Jaffe of City Coins, Cape Town, without whose assistance and encouragement this book would never have been published. To my long-suffering wife, Barbara, thank you for your support and patience.

Father and Son Awards

There were three father/son awards, two of which relate to the Anglo-Boer War:

Major Charles JS Gough, Indian Mutiny 1857-8, and Bt./Major John E Gough, Somaliland, 1904.

Lieut (later Field Marshal Earl) Roberts, Bengal Artillery, who received the VC for saving the life of an Indian trooper in 1858; and Lieut Frederick Roberts who received a posthumous award in 1899 for attempting to save the guns at Colenso.

Captain (later Lieut-General) Walter Congreve, Rifle Brigade, who survived the attempt to save the Colenso guns in 1899; and his son, Brigade Major Billy Congreve, who received a posthumous award for gallantry on the Western Front in July 1916. At the time his father commanded the XIII Corps.

Other titles by the Author

For Valour, the history of Southern Africa's Victoria Cross Heroes (1973)

Die Uys Geskiedenis (1974)

Heidelbergers of the Boer War (1981)

Delville Wood (1983)

Longueval (1986)

The Comrades (1987)

Rollcall, the Delville Wood Story (1991)

Cross of Honour (1992)

South African Military Who's Who (1992)

Bushman Soldiers, their Alpha and Omega (1993)

Survivors of Africa's Oceans (1993)

Tourists' Guide to the Comoros (1994)

Rearguard, the life and times of Piet Uys (1998)

Table of Contents

South Africa circa 1900

Key

---   Borders

——   Railway line

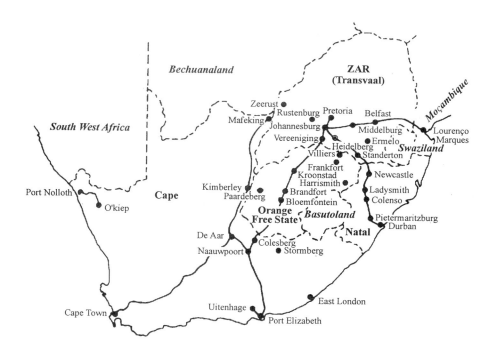

Introduction

The Victoria Cross is the highest award for valour which can be awarded to British and Commonwealth forces. Since its inception in 1854 it has been bestowed 1,354 times. It can only be awarded for acts in the presence of the enemy, making the chances of surviving a VC act one in ten.

During the First Anglo-Boer War (or Transvaal War of Independence) six VCs were awarded. These and the DCMs won were virtually the only medals awarded for that war as no campaign medal was issued. The reason for the inclusion of these VCs with those of the Second Anglo-Boer War is because the same opponents fought over the same terrain – and similar acts of bravery were performed.

The Boers had no gallantry awards – in fact they had no medals at all until they were promulgated in 1920. The *Dekoratie voor Trouwe Dienst* (DSO) was for officers only whereas the *Anglo-Boere Oorlogmedalje* was the campaign medal for the Second Anglo-Boer War. It is unfortunate that the Boers did not similarly honour their heroes; men such as Christiaan de Wet, Danie Theron and the Rev J D Kestell would certainly have qualified for an award such as the VC.

There were 78 VCs awarded for the Anglo-Boer War. An analyses of these appears in the appendices. When *For Valour, the History of Southern Africa's Victoria Cross Heroes* was published in 1973 there were fewer reference sources, hence some changes which appear in this book.

Each VC recipient's age is noted with his name and his biography is presented together with his citation. The OD&M (Orders, Decorations and Medals) ascribed to each person are prepared to the best of my knowledge and belief. Particulars of the 'Queen's Scarf' recipients are included because of their similarity to some VCs – an award instituted by Queen Victoria, to be awarded to the bravest men of each country, by election, during the war.

Any errors are regretted. All corrections and proposed additions are welcome. In the spirit of reconciliation which has pervaded South Africa during the past ten years, one can but acknowledge the bravery displayed by men in battles of the past.

Ian Uys
Knysna
2000

Monarchs of the Empire

(Knysna Library)

Victoria 1819 - 1901
Reigned 1837 - 1901

(Painting by Sir Luke Fildes)

Edward VII 1841 - 1910
Reigned 1901 - 1910

Queen's & King's South Africa Medals

VCs of the First Anglo-Boer War

1881

MURRAY, James, 23
Lance Corporal, 94th Regiment

(Creagh)

He was born at St Michaels, Cork City, Ireland in Feb 1857. Murray served in the 2nd Bn Connaught Rangers (94th Regt). At dawn on January 16, 1881, a mounted column under Col Gildea left Pretoria. About seven miles out he was informed that a number of Boers occupied a strong position on the slopes of Elandsfontein Ridge.

One of the British nine-pounders bombarded the ridge for 20 minutes, then the 94th Regiment advanced. They were subjected to heavy rifle fire by the Boers. Colonel Bellairs CB arrived and ordered Gildea to withdraw. As the column left it was found that three men were missing, believed to be lying wounded at the base of the ridge.

Two men, L/Cpl James Murray of the Connaught Rangers and Private John Danaher of Nourse's Horse, rode forward. Murray's horse was shot, so they proceeded on foot.

Citation: For gallant conduct (with Trooper Danaher of Nourse's Horse) during an engagement with the Boers at Elandsfontein on the 16th January 1881, in advancing for 500 yards, under a very heavy fire from a party of about sixty Boers, to bring out of action a private of the 21st Foot, who had been severely wounded; in attempting which L/Corpl Murray was himself severely wounded. (LG March 14, 1882).

Murray stooped to raise Pte Byrne's head and, while kneeling, was shot in his right side. He collapsed beside the man he had come to rescue. Murray and the wounded man, Davis, were taken prisoner and well treated by the Boers. They were permitted to return to Pretoria with the body of Private Byrne under a flag of truce. Davis died five days later. According to Lehmann, "Murray survived a severe wound to be personally invested with the honour by the Queen". Murray died at Dublin on July 19, 1942, aged 85. In 1961 his daughter-in-law presented his medals to the National Army Museum.

OD&M: VC, SAGS 1879 (Clasp 1879), Coronation Medal 1937.

DANAHER, John, 20
Trooper, Nourse's Horse

He was born at Limerick, Ireland, on June 25, 1860. Danaher came to the Transvaal where he joined a colonial unit, raised by Captain Nourse and Capt A Woolls-Sampsons for the defence of Pretoria, with a strength of 60 men.

(Creagh)

Citation: See J Murray (LG March 14, 1882). In the original citation his name was spelt Danagher.

Realising that it would be useless for Danaher to proceed with the rescue on his own and in the face of the heavy fire, Murray ordered him to take the carbines and retire. Danaher stood for a few moments over his wounded companions, fired a few shots at the enemy, then gathered up all the rifles and calmly marched back to his lines.

After the Siege Danaher joined the 2nd Connaught Rangers in April 1881. His VC was presented to him in August 1882 at the Curragh Camp by Earl Spencer KG. Sergeant Danaher was recommended for meritorious service by General Sir Archibald Hunter, before retiring from the army.

Six of his sons served in World War I; one died of wounds received at Gallipoli, a second was wounded and a third was taken prisoner. John Danaher, the only man to win a VC while serving in a South African unit during the Transvaal War of Independence, died in Ireland on January 9, 1919, aged 58 years.

His medals were given to the National Army Museum in 1971 by his daughter-in-law, Mrs Dorothy Danagher of Southsea, Hampshire.

OD&M: VC, Long Service and Good Conduct Medal (Victorian).

HILL (later Hill-Walker), Alan Richard, 21
Lieut, 2nd Bn, 58th Northamptons

(The Register)

Born on July 12, 1859, at Maunby Hall, near Thirsk, Yorkshire, he was the eldest son of the Chief Constable of the Yorkshire North Riding. He joined the North York Rifles in 1877 and the 58th Regt in 1879, with which he served in the Zulu War and the Transvaal War. Lieutenant Hill took part in the Battle of Laing's Nek, on the Natal/Transvaal border. This was the last occasion on which British colours were carried into battle. Some historians contend that it was at Tel-el-Kebir the following year, or by the 2nd KOYLI in Burma in 1942.

Colonel Deane and various staff officers led the 58th Regt up the steep hillside against a prepared Boer position. Deane was shot off his charger and mortally wounded. With their colours flying and men dropping everywhere the redcoats surged up to the Boer defences, then were driven back. Major Essex, a survivor of the Battle of Isandlwana, then ordered a bugler to sound the retreat.

During the retiral Lieut Baillie, who carried the black regimental colours, was wounded. Lieutenant Peel, who carried the other colours, tried to assist him, but Baillie shouted, "Never mind me, save the colours." Peel then fell into an antbear hole and a sergeant, thinking him dead, retrieved both colours and took them to safety.

Citation: For gallant conduct at the action of Laing's Nek on the 28th January 1881, in having, after the retreat was ordered, remained behind and endeavoured to carry out of action Lieut Baillie, of the same corps, who was lying on the ground severely wounded. Being unable to lift that officer into the saddle, he carried him in his arms until Lieut Baillie was shot dead. Lieutenant Hill than brought a wounded man out of action on his horse, after which he returned and rescued another, all these acts being performed under a heavy fire. (LG March 14, 1882).

Hill was present at the actions at Ingogo and Majuba, and was severely wounded during the latter. According to Lehmann, "Not only did Hill receive the Victoria Cross, but his horse was posthumously honoured by having two of its hoofs mounted in silver, later to be used as ashtrays in the 58th mess."

He remained in South Africa until 1885, then served in Bangalore and Mandalay. In 1897 as a major he served in the Tirah Campaign. He married Muriel Walker, had two sons and assumed the additional name of Walker in

1902.

His elder son, Gerald, was a major with the Northamptons in 1940, the year that his younger son, Lieut-Commander Thomas Hill-Walker RN was killed in action. Hill-Walker died at Thirsk, Yorkshire, on April 21, 1944, aged 84 years.

OD&M: VC, SAGS 1879 (Clasp 1879), IGS (Clasp Tirah 1897).

DOOGAN, John, 27
Private, 1st Dragoon Guards.

He was born at Augrim, County Galway, Ireland in March 1853. Doogan joined a cavalry regiment and became the batman of Major Brownlow.

Citation: On January 28, 1881, at Laing's Nek. During the charge of the mounted men, Private Doogan, servant to Major Brownlow, 1st Dragoon Guards, seeing that officer (whose horse had been

(The Register)

shot) dismounted and among the Boers, rode up and (though himself severely wounded) dismounted and pressed Major Brownlow to take his horse, receiving another wound while trying to induce him to accept it. (LG March 14, 1882).

Private Doogan was awarded the VC and discharged on pension. He and his wife, Mary, had two sons, Jack and Dick, who were both killed in World War I. His wife died in 1924 and in 1933 Doogan remarried Bessie Evans from Wales.

In March 1926 Major-General William Brownlow, 84, was knocked down by a motor car and died at Eveley, Bordon, Hampshire. He left an annuity of £20 to Doogan, from an estate of £41,436.

He lived largely in Cork, Ireland, however died at Folkestone, Kent on Jan 24, 1940, and is buried in the Military Cemetery at Shorncliffe, Kent. He bequeathed his medals to the 1st (King's) Dragoon Guards.

OD&M: VC, Coronation Medals 1902, 1911 and 1937.

OSBORNE, James, 23
Private, Northamptonshire Regiment.

He was born at Wiggington, Tring, Hertfordshire on
April 13, 1857. Osborne served with the 2nd Bn, 58th
Northamptons, which garrisoned Wakkerstroom
during the Transvaal War of Independence. The town
had had a variety of names, initially Uysenburg, it
became Marthinus Wesselstroom then
Wakkerstroom.

(The Register)

The British garrison, consisting of two companies
(120 men) of the 94th Regt under Capt Saunders, held a small fort about a mile
north of the town. It also held the town with 30 men in the Dutch church.
Captain Saunders spread a rumour that the area around the town was heavily
mined, so the Boers never came near, though skirmishes between mounted
parties did take place.

Citation: For his gallant conduct at Wesselstroom, on the 22nd February 1881,
in riding, under a heavy fire, towards a party of 42 Boers, picking up Private
Mayes, who was lying wounded, and carrying him safely into camp. (LG
March 14, 1882).

During the investment of Wakkerstroom three soldiers were wounded, of
whom two later died. Osborne married Rhoda Collier at Wiggington in Sep
1883. He retired from the army after serving six years with the Colours and
five years on Reserve. Osborne died aged 70 near Tring on Feb 2, 1928, and is
buried at Wiggington.

On Dec 19, 1941, when the Japanese attacked Hong Kong, CSM John
Osborne commanded the rearguard and directed the fire of the Bren guns.
When a grenade was thrown at his party he deliberately fell on it to shield them
and was killed. His bravery was reported in 1946 by Sergt Pugsley of his party,
who had been taken prisoner by the Japanese.

O,D&M: VC, SAGS 1879 (Clasp 1879).

FARMER, Joseph John, 26
Provisional L/Corporal, Army Hospital Corps

Born in London on May 5, 1854, he left school when ten years old and went to sea. In 1878 Farmer contracted smallpox and was hospitalised at Hampstead Heath, London. After restraining a delirious patient he was employed as a porter. After the Zulu War Battle of Isandlwana he joined the Army Hospital Corps in Feb 1879 and, after a course in anatomy and ambulance work, went with reinforcements to South Africa.

(Wilkins)

Farmer helped at Pietermaritzburg with the Zulu War wounded of the Ulundi Battle, then served at Newcastle before going with a field hospital to the front. During the 1st Anglo-Boer War Farmer almost drowned when crossing the Ingogo River which was in flood.

Farmer accompanied General Colley's force, which did a night march up Majuba Mountain, overlooking the Boer camp near the Transvaal/Natal border.

At dawn the Boers saw the British on the crest of the hill and began a three-pronged attack. Their superior fire-power soon told and the Highlanders had to fall back as the Boers fought their way to the summit. General Colley was shot, and according to Lehmann, "Some said that the twelve-year-old son of Piet Uys did it".

In the hospital area Surgeon Landon and two assistants were hit. Landon made an unsuccessful attempt to halt the firing. While lying paralysed with a bullet in his spine he ordered L/Cpl Farmer to wave a triangular bandage to indicate that it was a hospital area. Farmer, who was slightly wounded, stood up and vigorously waved the bandage.

Citation: For conspicuous bravery during the engagements with the Boers at the Majuba Mountain, on the 27th February 1881, when he showed a spirit of self-abnegation and an example of cool courage which cannot be too highly commended. While the Boers closed with the British troops near the Wells, Cpl Farmer held a white flag over the wounded, and when the arm holding the flag was shot through, he called out that he had 'another'. He then raised the flag with the other arm, and continued to do so until that also was shot through. (London Gazette May 17, 1881).

He was initially shot through the hand, then through his other arm near the elbow. Some older Boers then stopped the firing and held Landon up so that he could give Farmer, who was in agony, an injection of morphine. The British suffered a resounding defeat, having six officers and 90 men killed as compared to the Boers' two killed. It was the primary reason for the peace treaty which followed.

Farmer's VC was presented by Queen Victoria at Osborne on August 9, 1881. Owing to his wounds Farmer left the service and joined the Corps of Commissionaires, then became a house painter in London. He married and had a son. He died at Northwood, London, on June 30, 1930, and is buried at Brompton Cemetery, London, where his memorial stone is a boulder from Majuba Mountain, presented by the Durban Light Infantry.

OD&M: VC, SAGS 1879 (Clasp 1879).

1899

FITZCLARENCE, Charles, 34
Captain, The Royal Fusiliers.

(With the Flag)

Born at Bishopscourt, County Kildare, Ireland on May 8, 1865, he was the son of the Hon George Fitzclarence, RN, and the great-grandson of King William IV. One of his uncles was killed at the Redan in the Crimea. Fitzclarence was educated at Eton and Wellington and commissioned in the Royal Fusiliers (City of London Regt) in 1886.

After serving in the Khartoum Campaign Fitzclarence was promoted captain in April 1898. That month he married Violet Churchill, a cousin of Winston Churchill, and they had a son and a daughter. He was sent to South Africa on special service in July 1899 and was present during the Siege of Mafeking, where he earned the nickname 'The Demon'.

Citation: On the 14th Oct 1899, Capt Fitzclarence went with his squadron of the Protectorate Regiment, consisting of only partially trained men, who had never been in action, to the assistance of an armoured train which had gone out from Mafeking. The enemy were in greatly superior numbers, and the squadron was for a time surrounded, and it looked as if nothing could save them from being shot down. Captain Fitzclarence, however, by his personal coolness and courage, inspired the greatest confidence in his men, and by his bold and efficient handling of them, not only succeeded in relieving the armoured train, but inflicted a heavy defeat on the Boers, who lost fifty killed and a large number of wounded; his own losses being two killed and fifteen wounded. The moral effect of this blow had a very important bearing on subsequent encounters with the Boers. On the 27th Oct 1899, Capt Fitzclarence led his squadron from Mafeking across the open, and made a night attack with the bayonet on one of the enemy's trenches. A hand-to-hand fight took place in the trench, while a heavy fire was concentrated on it from the rear. The enemy was driven out with heavy loss. Captain Fitzclarence was the first man into the position, and accounted for four of the enemy with his sword. The British lost six killed and nine wounded. Captain Fitzclarence was himself slightly wounded. With reference to these two actions Major-

General Baden-Powell states that had this officer not shown an extraordinary spirit and fearlessness, the attacks would have been failures, and we would have suffered heavy loss both in men and prestige. On the 26th Dec 1899, during the action of Game Tree, near Mafeking, Capt Fitzclarence again distinguished himself by his coolness and courage, and was again wounded severely through the leg. (LG July 6, 1900).

On formation of the Irish Guards in October 1900 Fitzclarence was transferred to that regiment and promoted major. He served as brigade-major until Feb 1901. From 1903-6 he was brigade major of the 5th Brigade at Aldershot. He was given command of the 1st Bn Irish Guards in 1909.

On outbreak of the Great War Fitzclarence commanded the 29th Brigade, then was given command of the First Guards Brigade in France. On October 31 during the 1st Battle of Ypres he rallied the Worcester Regt and directed a counter-attack which saved the line.

Brigadier-General Fitzclarence was killed while leading the 1st Guards Brigade against the Prussian Guard at Polygon Wood, Zonnebeke, east of Ypres during a night attack on November 11/12, 1914. He is commemorated on the Menin Gate Memorial, Belgium. His medals were sold by Sothebys in 1990 for £38,000.

OD&M: VC, QSA (Def of Maf, Tvl, OFS), 1914 Star, BWM, AVM (MID), Coronation Medal 1911.

MEIKLEJOHN, Matthew Fontaine Maury, 28
Captain, Gordon Highlanders

(Creagh)

He was born on Nov 27, 1870, the son of a professor and educated at Edinburgh. He was named after Matthew Fontaine Maury (1806-1873), an American Naval officer and hydrographer. Meiklejohn joined the Gordon Highlanders in India in June 1891 and four years later took part in the relief of Chitral. He saw further action at Dargai, where he was slightly wounded, and Tirah.

On outbreak of the war in South Africa the Gordons were shipped to Natal. General French attacked the Boers at Elandslaagte at dawn on the 21st October, and surprised the Boers under Gen Kock. Colonel Ian Hamilton then brought up reinforcements by train, the Manchesters, Devons and Gordon Highlanders supported by the Imperial Light Horse. Five companies of the 2nd Gordon Highlanders under Col Dick-Cunyngham VC were among the reinforcements.

The attack commenced at 4.30 pm. The Devons were pinned down by Boer fire at 800 yards, then the Manchesters, Gordons and ILH attacked on the right flank. The mixed force swept up the hill at dusk and took the crest.

The casualties among the Gordons and the Imperial Light Horse were very heavy as they crowded together at the gaps in the fences. Half the officers of the Gordons were dead or disabled, including Col Dick-Cunyngham who was wounded in two places.

Colonel Ian Hamilton noticed some Boers with a flag of truce, so ordered the 'cease fire' to be sounded. General Kock then led some 40-50 Boers in a counter-attack, which forced them back 100 yards.

According to the Times History "Ian Hamilton sprang forward, shouting wildly to his men that the guns were coming up to help (For his conduct in rallying the men Colonel Hamilton was recommended by General French for the Victoria Cross, and would no doubt have received it if it had not been considered inadvisable to set a precedent by conferring a decoration for purely personal valour on an officer in the position of a brigadier).

"Lieutenant Meiklejohn, of the Gordons, rushed to the front rallying the disconcerted groups, until he fell desperately wounded in half a dozen places (For his conduct on this occasion Lieut Meiklejohn received his Victoria Cross)."

Citation: At the battle of Elandslaagte, on the 21st Oct 1899, after the main Boer position had been captured, some of the men of the Gordon Highlanders, when about to advance, were exposed to a heavy cross-fire, and, having lost their leaders, commenced to waver. Seeing this, Capt Meiklejohn rushed to the front and called on the Gordons to follow him. By his conspicuous bravery and fearless example he rallied the men and led them against the enemy's position, where he fell, desperately wounded in four places. (London Gazette July 20, 1900).

Meiklejohn was taken to Ladysmith where his right arm was amputated, almost at the shoulder. He survived his wounds and the siege, then was decorated by Queen Victoria at Windsor Castle in Dec 1900. In 1901 he was Garrison Adjutant at St Helena.

Meiklejohn married Vera Marshall in 1904 and they had a son and two daughters. He then served on the General Staff at Army HQ, where he received his majority, then became an officer-instructor at the Royal Military College, Sandhurst.

On June 28, 1913, Meiklejohn was present at an inspection of the University of London's Officers Training Corps at Rotten Row, Hyde Park, when his horse was frightened by the band and bolted. In order to avoid some children and their nursemaid he selflessly steered his horse into the steel railings. He died of his injuries at the Middlesex Hospital on July 4, aged 42 years, and is buried in Brookwood Cemetery. The king and queen were represented at his funeral.

OD&M: VC, IGS (Tirah 1897-8), QSA (Elandslaagte, Defence of Ladysmith), Coronation Medals 1902 and 1911.

ROBERTSON, William, 34
Sergeant-Major, 2nd Bn. The Gordon Highlanders

Born on Feb 27, 1865, at Greyfriars, Dumfrieshire, Scotland, he joined the army in Dec 1884. In 1891 he married Sara Ferris of Belfast and they had three sons and a daughter. After serving with the Gordons in India he arrived in Natal with his regiment two days before the ultimatum expired.

(Creagh)

Citation: At the Battle of Elandslaagte, on the 21st Oct 1899, during the final advance on the enemy's position, this warrant officer led each successive rush, exposing himself fearlessly to the enemy's artillery and rifle fire to encourage the men. After the main position had been captured, he led a small party to seize the Boer camp. Though exposed to a deadly cross-fire from the enemy's rifles, he gallantly held the position captured, and continued to encourage the men until he was wounded in two places. (LG July 20, 1900).

Robertson was recommended for the VC by Brig Ian Hamilton, who said, "No better VC was ever won than William Robertsons's". He was commissioned before being decorated by Queen Victoria in Aug 1900 at Osborne. During and after World War I Lieut-Col Robertson was Recruiting Staff Officer for Edinburgh.
   He became widely known for his work on behalf of disabled ex-servicemen through the British Legion. He died at Edinburgh on December 6, 1949, aged 84 years and was buried at Portobello Cemetery.

OD&M: VC, CBE, CGS, QSA (Elandslaagte, Ladysmith, Cape), 1914-15 Star, BWM, AVM, Coronation Medals 1911 and 1937, Legion d' Honour (France).

MULLINS, Charles Herbert, 30
Captain, Imperial Light Horse, SA Forces

He was born on 28 June 1869, at Grahamstown, Cape. The son of Rev Canon Mullins, he was educated at St Andrew's College and in 1888 studied law at Oxford. He graduated in 1891 and two years later was called to the Bar. Mullins played rugby for Keble and was a member of the athletic team. His brother, Robert George, represented the British Isles at rugby during their tour of South Africa in 1896.

(Uys)

Mullins returned to South Africa and practised in Johannesburg, where he served on the Reform Committee and was one of the founders of the Imperial Light Horse (ILH). During the Battle of Elandslaagte Col Scott-Chisholme was wounded, then killed as he was being assisted to safety. Mullins was the senior ILH officer present at the final charge.

Citation: Captain Charles Herbert Mullins, Captain, ILH, and Robert Johnston, Captain, ILH. On the 21st October, 1899, at Elandslaagte, at a most critical moment, the advance being momentarily checked by a very severe fire at point-blank range, these two officer very gallantly rushed forward under this heavy fire and rallied the men, thus enabling the flanking movement which decided the day to be carried out. On this occasion Captain Mullins was wounded. (LG February 12, 1901).

Mullins contracted enteric while besieged in Ladysmith, but survived. He was promoted major and took part in the Relief of Mafeking under Col Mahon DSO. They were ambushed on Sunday, May 13, 1900, at Maritzane (Koodoosrand). Mullins was riddled with bullets and became a cripple. He was decorated by King Edward VII at St James Palace in July 1901 and created a CMG that year. In 1902 he returned to his practice, married Norah Haslam and they had two sons and a daughter.

In 1913 he was appointed President of the High Courts of Swaziland and of Bechuanaland (Botswana). He died aged 46 years in Johannesburg on Empire Day, May 24, 1916, and is buried in Grahamstown.

OD&M: VC, CMG, QSA (Elandslaagte, Defence of Ladysmith, Relief of Mafeking), KSA (SA01, SA02), Coronation Medal 1911.

JOHNSTON, Robert, 27
Captain, Imperial Light Horse, SA Forces

He was born at Laputa, Donegal, Ireland on August
13, 1872. The son of a QC he went to school on the
Isle of Man, then joined the army at the age of 18.
From 1890-4 Johnston served in the Royal
Inniskilling Fusiliers. He represented Ireland at rugby
in 1893 and toured South Africa with the British Isles
team in 1896. Johnston and a fellow team mate,
Tommy Crean, remained after the tour and played
rugby for Wanderers and the Transvaal.

(Uys)

On outbreak of the SA War he was commissioned in the Imperial Light
Horse. Robert Johnston was promoted captain before the Battle of
Elandslaagte. He and Lieut Brabant supported Capt Mullins in checking the
retreat at a crucial stage.

Citation: See Captain C H Mullins (LG February 12, 1901).

Johnston was seriously wounded at Ladysmith and retired from active service.
He was decorated with the VC by King Edward VII at St James Palace,
London, in July 1901. In 1902 he was commandant of a concentration camp at

(Light Horse Regiment)

Battle of Elandslaagte.

Middelburg and in 1903 district land commissioner of the Eastern Transvaal. He returned to Ireland and in 1911 joined the prison service.

During 1914-15 Major Johnston was commandant of the POW Camp at Oldcastle, then was appointed governor of HM Convict Prison at Maryborough. In 1918 he was appointed as a resident magistrate. Johnston was very fond of fishing and golf, though he farmed and bred thoroughbred cattle. He died at Kilkenny, Eire, on March 24, 1950, aged 77 years.

OD&M: VC, QSA (Elandslaagte, Defence of Ladysmith), KSA (SA01, SA02), 1914-15 Star, BWM, AVM, Coronation Medals 1911 and 1937.

NORWOOD, John, 23
Lieut, 5th Dragoon Guards

(Creagh)

He was born at Beckenham, Kent, on September 8, 1876, and educated at Beckenham, Rugby and Oxford. Norwood joined the 5th Dragoons (Princess Charlotte of Wales's) in Feb 1899. On outbreak of the Anglo-Boer War he was best-man at his cousin, Una Brown's wedding to Charlie Adams in Durban. He left for the front immediately after the ceremony and took part in the Battle of Elandslaagte.

On Sep 4, 1900, Norwood wrote, "I had on a mackintosh and a blue cardigan vest tied round my neck a splendid charging kit for a dragoon. We soon got into line and went away - left shoulders - and we had them right across our line. Of the rest I have the very vaguest recollection a vision of Watson cocking his mauser, a crowd of Boers with their hands up and arms cast away.

"Meanwhile I steadily let off my mauser [revolver], until my eye caught a Boer on a white horse getting away, so I pursued, but Wynne of the 5th Lancers caught him first with a nasty sword over the head. Then I saw another Boer and I stupidly went after him, but couldn't catch him ..."

During the Battle of Ladysmith at 10.30 pm on October 29, Col Carleton led a column northwards up the Bell Spruit toward Nicholson's Nek, then found himself cut off on Tchrengula Hill. His mules stampeded, losing him his mountain guns. General White tried in vain to get a message through ordering him to retire.

According to the Times History, "It was impossible for mounted messengers to ride up the valley of the Bell Spruit, now completely commanded by the Boers. An officer's patrol of the 5th Dragoon Guards had made an attempt earlier in the morning to get through to Carleton, but in spite of the gallantry of Lieutenant Norwood and Private Sibthorp (for which they received the Victoria Cross and Distinguished Conduct Medal) respectively, had been compelled to return.

"An attempt to send through Kaffir runners proved equally unsuccessful. A heliographic message, ordering Carleton to 'retire as opportunity offered', was not sent for some time, as the heliograph at Bell's Farm failed to elicit any answer to its call from the heliographs that Carleton was supposed to have with him."

During the patrol Private Mouncer had been hit by a bullet in the throat. While Sec-Lieut Norwood carried him out, Private Sibthorpe returned to assist him.

Citation: On the 30th October 1899, this officer went out from Ladysmith in charge of a small patrol of the 5th Dragoon Guards. They came under a heavy fire from the enemy, who were posted on a ridge in great force. The patrol, which had arrived within about 600 yards of the ridge, then retired at full speed. One man dropped, and Sec-Lieut Norwood galloped back about 300 yards through heavy fire, dismounted, and picking up the fallen trooper, carried him out of fire on his back, at the same time leading his horse with one hand. The enemy kept up an incessant fire during the whole time that Sec-Lieut Norwood was carrying the man until he was quite out of range. (LG July 27, 1900).

Commandant Christiaan de Wet seized the northern part of the hill and brought a terrific fire down on Carleton's column. By 1.15 pm the white flag was hoisted and the Boers took the surrender. The British officially reported some 43 officers and 925 men as missing.

Norwood was promoted captain in the 5th Dragoons and awarded the VC, while Pvt Sibthorp got the DCM. In May 1901 the latter was dangerously wounded and evacuated to England. Norwood later served as adjutant to the Calcutta Light Horse. He joined the Reserve of Officers in 1911.

During the 1st World War Captain Norwood was killed during the Battle of the Marne on Sept 8, 1914, the day before his 38th birthday, at Sablonnieres, France. He is buried in the new communal cemetery. Norwood was the first VC recipient killed in World War I. There is a memorial to him in Peckham Church. His son, John, was to become a group captain in the RAF.

OD&M: VC, QSA (Defence of Ladysmith), KSA (SA 01, SA 02), 1914-15 Star, BWM, AVM, Coronation Medal 1911.

TOWSE, Ernest Beachcroft Beckwith, 35
Captain, Gordon Highlanders

Born on April 23, 1864, he was educated at
Wellington College. He joined the Gordon
Highlanders in Jan 1886. In 1892 he married Gertrude
Christie. Towse accompanied the Gordons to India
where in 1895 he served with the Chitral Relief Force,
at Malakand, on the North-West Frontier and in 1897-
8 at Tirah.

(Creagh)

In South Africa the western campaign under Lord
Methuen had seen his army advance despite fighting at Belmont, Graspan and
Modder River. After reorganising, he decided on a night advance and dawn
attack on the Boer positions at Magersfontein. He was unaware that the Boers
had entrenched themselves at the foot of the hill, so sent his troops into a
veritable slaughterhouse.

The Highland Brigade walked into a storm of fire at 4 am, and lost General
Wauchope. After 11 am Lord Methuen ordered forward six companies of the
Gordons under Col Downman to support the line directly opposite the
Magersfontein Kop and Boer trenches. Their attack died away 400 yards from
the Boer trenches.

Colonel Downman saw the British right flank retiring at 2 pm so assumed
incorrectly that a general retreat had been ordered. He ordered a retirement,
thereby causing the Highlanders heavy losses as they stood up and walked
back in the open veld.

According to the Times History, "Downman fell mortally wounded the
moment he rose to retire. Captain E B Towse, of the Gordons, with
conspicuous gallantry, stayed by his wounded colonel's side till Sergeant
Nelson and Lance-Corporal Hodgson came and helped to carry him back
under the heavy fire."

Citation: On the 11th Dec 1899, at the action of Magersfontein, Capt Towse
was brought to notice by his commanding officer for his gallantry and
devotion in assisting the late Colonel Downman, when mortally wounded, in
the retirement, and endeavouring, when close up to the front of the firing-line,
to carry Colonel Downman on his back; but finding this not possible, Capt
Towse supported him till joined by Colour-Sergt Nelson and L-Corpl.
Hodgson. On the 30th April, 1900, Capt Towse, with twelve men, took up a
position on the top of Mount Thaba, far away from support. A force of about
150 Boers attempted to seize the same plateau, neither party appearing to see
the other until they were but one hundred yards apart. Some of the Boers then
got within forty yards of Capt Towse and his party, and called on him to

surrender. He at once caused his men to open fire, and remained firing himself until severely wounded (both eyes shattered), thus succeeding in driving off the Boers. The gallantry of this officer in vigorously attacking the enemy (for he not only fired, but charged forward) saved the situation, notwithstanding the numerical superiority of the Boers. (LG July 6, 1900).

According to Sir Arthur Conan Doyle, "It was in this action, during the fighting on the hill, that Captain Towse, of the Gordons, though shot through the eyes and totally blind, encouraged his men to charge through a group of the enemy who had gathered round them."

Captain Towse was decorated by Queen Victoria at Windsor Castle in July 1900 and appointed Sergeant-at-Arms. The appointment was confirmed by King Edward in 1902. The following year Towse became one of the Hon Corps of Gentlemen-at-Arms. He became an expert typist and during the Great War he went to the front to type letters for wounded soldiers as Hon Staff Captain for Base Hospitals.

In 1921 he accompanied Field Marshal Earl Haig to South Africa to form an Empire League of ex-servicemen. Towse was in the Hon Corps of Gentlemen-at-Arms until 1939. He became a Knight of Grace of the Order of St John of Jerusalem and Chairman of the Grand Council of the Comrades of the Great War. Towse was knighted KCVO. Sir Beachcroft Towse died at Goring-on-Thames, Berkshire, on June 21, 1948, aged 84 years. His medals are in the regimental museum at Aldershot.

OD&M: VC, KCVO, CBE, India Medal (Tirah 1897-8), QSA (Modder R, Rel of Kimb, Paardeberg), 1914-15 Star, BWM, AVM, Knight of Grace of the Order of St John, Coronation Medals 1911 and 1937.

SHAUL, John David Francis, 26
Corporal, 1ˢᵗ Bn, The Highland Light Infantry

Born at King's Lynn, Norfolk, on Sept 11, 1873, his father, Sgt John Shaul of the Royal Scots was a veteran of the Crimea and China (1860). After attending the Duke of York's School, in 1888, aged 15, Shaul joined the Highland Light Infantry. He was on active service in Crete during the fighting in 1898. The following year his regiment was sent to South Africa.

(Wilkins)

Citation: On the 11th Dec 1899, during the Battle of Magersfontein, Corpl Shaul was observed, not only by the officers of his own battalion, but by several officers of other regiments, to perform several specific acts of bravery. Corporal Shaul was in charge of stretcher- bearers; but at one period of the battle he was seen encouraging men to advance across the open. He was most conspicuous during the day in dressing men's wounds, and in one case he came, under a heavy fire, to a man who was lying wounded in the back, and with the utmost coolness and deliberation sat down beside the wounded man and proceeded to dress his wound. Having done this, he got up and went quietly to another part of the field. This act of gallantry was performed, under a continuous and heavy fire, as coolly and quietly as if there had been no enemy near. (LG Sept 28, 1900).

Shaul was decorated by HRH the Duke of Cornwall & York at Pietermaritzburg in Aug 1901. He was later promoted band sergeant. In 1904 Shaul was stationed in Khartoum. During his service he was a member of the Independent Order of Good Templars. He left his battalion in Lucknow, India, in 1909, having served for 21 years.

Shaul came to work on the East Rand Premier Goldmine at Boksburg, Transvaal. He became bandmaster of the Imperial Light Horse and during World War I served with the 5th SAI in East Africa. He was invalided home due to dysentery. He had three sons, one of whom was killed in a flying accident at Sonderwater, Transvaal, during World War II. Shaul died at Boksburg, South Africa, on September 14, 1953, aged 80 years, and is buried in the Boksburg Cemetery.

OD&M: VC, QSA (Three clasps), KSA (SA01, SA02), 1914-15 Star, BWM, AVM, Coronation Medals 1911, 1937 and 1953.

DOUGLAS, Henry Edward Manning, 24
Lieut, Royal Army Medical Corps

He was born at Gillingham, Kent, on July 11, 1875, although his father, George Douglas, was of Kingston, Jamaica. Douglas joined the Medical Branch of the Army in July 1899.

Citation: On the 11th Dec 1899, during the action at Magersfontein, Lieut Douglas showed great gallantry

(Wilkins)

18

and devotion, under a very severe fire, in advancing in the open and attending to Capt Gordon, Gordon Highlanders, who was wounded, and also attending to Major Robinson and other wounded men under a fearful fire. Many similar acts of devotion and gallantry were performed by Lieut Douglas on the same day. (LG March 29, 1901).

He was created a Companion of the DSO, gazetted on April 18, 1901, in recognition of his services in South Africa.

In July, 1900, Capt Gordon, whom Douglas assisted, was himself to earn a VC. Douglas was promoted captain in July 1902, before returning to England. From Oct 1903 he served in Somaliland, being present at the Battle of Jidballi. In 1906 Douglas served at Army HQ and the following year was stationed at Lucknow, India. He was promoted major in 1911, lieut-colonel in 1915 and created a CMG in 1916.

Douglas was commandant of the Royal Army Medical College from 1926-9, then Deputy Director Medical Services, Southern Command, India, until 1933. Major-General Douglas died at Droitwich, Worcestershire, on February 14, 1939. His decorations and medals are at the RAMC Headquarters at Millbank, London.

OD&M: VC, CB, CMG, DSO, QSA, 1914-15 Star, BWM, AVM, Coronation Medals 1911 and 1937, Order of St Sava, Serbia (1916), Croix de Guerre avec Palme (France).

SCHOFIELD, Harry Norton, 34.
Captain, Royal Field Artillery

He was born at Ashton-under-Lyne, Lancashire, on January 29, 1865, and attended the Royal Military Academy at Woolwich. Commissioned in the Royal Artillery in 1884, he was promoted captain by 1893. Schofield served as ADC to General Buller at Colenso.

(Wilkins)

General Buller opened his attack on the Boer centre on the Tugela River. At 5.30 am on December 15 the British heavy guns opened up, to be followed at 6 am by Colonel Long galloping his medium field guns (14th and 66th Batteries) to within 1,200 yards of the enemy. His gunners began to fall under a terrific volume of fire from the Boers. At 6.30 am Long was wounded and his surviving gunners took shelter in a large donga, leaving the guns unattended.

Citation: At Colenso on 15 December, 1899. When the detachments serving the guns of the 14th and 66th Batteries, Royal Field Artillery, had all been killed, wounded or driven from them by infantry fire at close range, Capt Schofield went out when the first attempt was made to extricate the guns, and assisted in withdrawing the two that were saved. Note: In consequence of the above, the appointment of this officer to the Distinguished Service Order, which was notified in the London Gazette of the 19th April, 1901, is cancelled. (LG August 30, 1901).

According to the Times History (Vol II p 452) Gen Buller at first refused to recommend Schofield for the VC on the ground that he had been told to make the attempt. Mr St John Brodrick decided that a VC could be gained for deeds performed under orders. Accordingly his award was gazetted 18 months after the other Colenso VC's.

Schofield saw action at Spion Kop, Vaal Krantz and Pieter's Hill then, after the relief of Ladysmith, at Laing's Nek and operations in the Eastern Transvaal at Belfast and Lydenburg. He was promoted major in 1900 and later served in the Corps of Gentlemen-at-Arms.

From 1914 he served on the British Remount Commission in Canada and America, then as commandant of Lines of Communication of the BEF. He married Dorothy Vere in June 1917 and retired the following year with the rank of lieut-colonel. Lieut-Col Schofield died in London on October 10, 1931, aged 66, and is buried in Putney Vale Cemetery. His medals were sold by Alec Kaplan, Johannesburg, in July 1985 and Sotheby's in Nov 1988.

OD&M: VC, QSA (Cape, Tug Hts, OFS, Rel of L, L Nek, Belf), KSA, 1914-15 Star, BWM, AVM, Coronation Medals 1902 and 1911.

CONGREVE, Walter Norris, 27
Captain, The Rifle Brigade (Prince Consort's Own)

He was born at Chatham, Kent, on November 20, 1862, educated at Harrow and joined the Rifle Brigade in 1885. By 1893 Congreve was a captain.

(Wilkins)

Citation: At Colenso on the 15th December, 1899, the detachments serving the guns of the 14th and 66th Batteries, Royal Field Artillery, had all been either killed, wounded, or driven from their guns by infantry fire at close range, and the guns were deserted. About 500 yards behind the guns was a donga, in which some of the few horses and drivers left alive were sheltered. The intervening space was swept with shell and rifle fire. Capt Congreve, Rifle Brigade, who was in the donga, assisted to hook a team into a limber, went out and assisted to limber up a gun. Being wounded, he took shelter, but seeing Lieut Roberts fall badly wounded, he went out and brought him in. Captain Congreve was shot through the leg, the toe of his boot, grazed on the elbow and shoulder, and his horse shot in three places. (LG Feb 3, 1900).

Congreve's tunic was torn to shreds by bullets. He married Celia la Touche in 1900 and had three sons. He was promoted major and became private secretary to Lord Kitchener. In Dec 1902 Congreve became ADC to the Duke of Connaught and the following year was made a Member of the Royal Victorian Order by the king.

Congreve was promoted major-general in 1915. One of his sons, Major William La Touche (Billy) Congreve was shot by a sniper near Delville Wood, in the Somme, in July 1916 and won a posthumous VC. Congreve was created a KCB in 1917 and promoted lieut-general in 1918. Sir Walter became governor of Malta and died while in office on February 26, 1927. He is buried at sea and commemorated by a stone pillar on the Maltese South Coast and by a tablet in Stow-by Chartley church in Staffordshire.

OD&M: VC, KCB, Cmdr of the Legion of Honour, QSA (7 clasps), KSA (SA01, SA02), 1914-15 Star, BWM, AVM, Coronation Medals 1911 and 1937, Order of St Anne of Russia (First Class).

REED, Hamilton Lyster, 30
Captain, 7th Battery, Royal Field Artillery

The son of Sir Andrew Reed, Inspector General of the Royal Irish Constabulary, Reed was born on May 23, 1869. He was educated at the Military Academy, Woolwich, and commissioned in 1888. By 1898 he was a captain. The following year he was involved in the Colenso debacle.

(Creagh)

Citation: Captain Reed who had heard of the difficulty, shortly afterwards brought down three teams from his battery to see if he could be of any use. He was wounded, as were five of the thirteen men who rode with him. One was

21

killed, and thirteen (including his own) out of twenty one horses were killed before he got half-way to the guns, and he was obliged to retire. (LG February 2, 1900).

Captain Reed was slightly wounded. He was presented with the VC by Gen Buller at Ladysmith on March 4, 1900. He became adjutant to the RFA, then DAAG on the staff of the GOC of the Orange River Colony. Reed took part in the fighting at Spion Kop, Vaal Krantz and Pieter's Hill, then at Laing's Nek before operations in the Transvaal. He also took part in operations in the ORC and was mentioned in despatches three times.

He was promoted major in 1904 and served on the General Staff, Army HQ from 1906-10. In 1911 Reed married Marjorie Olive and they had a son and two daughters. He served in the Balkan War from 1912-3. Colonel Reed served from 1914 and was created a CMG in 1916 and a CB in January 1918. By June 1919 he was a major-general. Reed died in London on March 7, 1931, aged 61.

His widow remarried a Mr Hannay. Reed's only son, Andrew Patrick, 26, served in the Royal Ulster Rifles and became a flying officer in the RAF. He was killed in action in May 1940.

OD&M: VC, CB, CMG, QSA (Six clasps), KSA (Two clasps), 1914-15 Star, BWM, AVM (MID seven times), Coronation Medals 1911 and 1937, Croix de Guerre.

ROBERTS, The Hon Frederick Sherston, 27
Lieut, King's Royal Rifle Corps

The son of Field Marshal Lord 'Bobs' Roberts VC, he was born at Umballa, India, on January 8, 1872. Freddy Roberts was educated at Eton and was immensely popular. He joined the KRRC at the age of 19, then served four years on active service on the North-West Frontier of India.

(Wilkins)

Roberts was ADC to Maj-Gen Sir Herbert Kitchener KCB KCMG in the Nile Expeditionary Force 1897-8. He was mentioned in despatches for the Battle of Omdurman. Roberts was serving on Gen Buller's staff at Colenso when volunteers were called for to save the guns.

Citation: Per Capt W N Congreve, plus: Lieut Roberts assisted Capt Congreve. He was wounded in three places. (LG Feb 3, 1900).

Roberts was mortally wounded and died on Dec 17, 1899. He is buried at Chieveley Station. In January 1900 his father was placed in command of all British forces in South Africa. The gun Lieut Roberts had tried to save was presented by the War Office to Lord Roberts and was used as the gun carriage when the latter was buried in 1916.

His and his father's medals are at the National Army Museum. There is a memorial to him in Winchester Cathedral and in the chapel at the Royal Military College, Sandhurst.

OD&M: VC, IGS 1854-95 (Clasp Waziristan 1894-95), India Medal (Clasp Relief of Chitral), Queen's Sudan Medal 1896-97, QSA being a first striking with dates 1899-1902 on the reverse (Clasp Relief of Ladysmith, Natal), Queen Victoria's Diamond Jubilee Medal 1897, Order of the Medidje, Turkey (Badge of the 4th Class), Khedive's Sudan Medal 1896-1908.

(With the Flag)

Death of Lieut Roberts.

BABTIE, William, 40, CMG
Major, Royal Army Medical Corps

He was born at Dumbarton, Scotland on May 7, 1859, and studied at the University of Glasgow to qualify as a doctor in 1880. He joined the Army Medical Corps the following year. From 1897-8 Major Babtie served in Crete as senior medical officer and was created a CMG in 1899. He was on the Staff of the Natal Army at Colenso when he heard the call for a surgeon to attend to the wounded near the abandoned guns.

(Creagh)

Citation: At Colenso on the 15th Dec 1899, the wounded of the 14th and 66th Batteries, Royal Field Artillery, were lying in an advanced donga close to the rear of the guns, without any medical officer to attend to them; and when a message was sent back asking for assistance, Major W Babtie, RAMC, rode up under a heavy rifle fire, his pony being hit three times. When he arrived at the donga, where the wounded were lying in a sheltered corner, he attended to them all, going from place to place exposed to the heavy rifle fire which greeted anyone who showed himself. Later on in the day Major Babtie went out with Capt Congreve to bring in Lieut Roberts, who was lying wounded on the veldt. This was under a heavy fire. (LG April 20, 1900).

He was promoted Lieut-Col and awarded the VC by Lord Roberts at Pretoria in Oct 1900. Babtie took part in the subsequent operations in Natal and the Eastern Transvaal. In 1903 he married Edith Barry of County Cork and they had a daughter. From 1901-6 he was Assistant Director-General Army Medical Services, then until 1910 Inspector of Medical Services. He was created a CB in 1912.

From 1914 Babtie was Director of Medical Services in India, then in the Mediterranean during the Dardanelles Campaign. In Jan 1916 he was created a KCMG and became Director, then in 1918 Inspector of Medical Services at the War Office. In June 1919 Lieut-General Babtie was created a KCB. He was honorary surgeon to the king and a Knight of Grace of the Order of St John of Jerusalem and an LLD of the University of Glasgow. Sir William died at Knocke, Belgium, on September 11, 1920, aged 61 years.

OD&M: VC, KCB, KCMG, QSA (Five clasps), 1914-15 Star, BWM, AVM, Coronation Medal 1911, Knight of Grace of the Order of St John of Jerusalem.

NURSE, George Edward, 26
Corporal, 66th Battery, Royal Field Artillery

(Wilkins)

He was born at Enniskillen, Ireland, on April 14, 1873. George Nurse studied at Guernsey, then joined the RA in London in January 1892 and served in Ireland until 1897. He proceeding to South Africa in December 1899. His unit was commanded by Major Foster, who served under Col Long.

Citation: Per Capt W N Congreve, plus: Lieut Roberts, King's Royal Rifle Corps, assisted Capt Congreve. He was wounded in three places. Corpl Nurse also assisted. (LG Feb 3, 1900).

Corporal Nurse was presented with his VC by Gen Buller at Ladysmith in March 1900. He and his wife, Kathleen, were to have a son, Charles T Colenso Nurse. In September 1915 Nurse was commissioned as a Temporary Sec-Lieutenant and served until 1916.

After the war he was on the cleaning staff at the Liverpool Custom House. Captain Nurse died at Liverpool, Lancashire, on November 25, 1945, aged 72, and is buried at Allerton Cemetery, Liverpool.

In 1991 Bombardier Stuart Colenso Nurse, 25, from Braintree, Essex, served with the Royal Artillery in the Gulf War. His great-grandfather's VC and medals were presented to his battery at Woolwich.

OD&M: VC, QSA, 1914-15 Star, BWM, AVM, Coronation Medals 1911 and 1937.

RAVENHILL, George, 27
Private, 2nd Bn, Royal Scots Fusiliers

(Wilkins)

Born at Birmingham on Feb 21, 1872, he joined the 1st Bn, Royal Scots Fusiliers in 1889 and served in India for six years. Ravenhill transferred to the 2nd Bn for service in South Africa and was present at Colenso.

Citation: At Colenso, on the 15th Dec 1899, Private Ravenhill went several times, under a heavy fire, from his sheltered position as one of the escort to the guns to assist the officers and drivers who were trying to withdraw the guns of the 14th and 66th Batteries, the Royal Field Artillery, when the detachments serving them had all been killed, wounded or driven from them by infantry fire at close range, and helped to limber up one of the guns that were saved. (LG June 4, 1901).

The citation was incorrectly headed 'Ravenhill, Private C'. Private Ravenhill's later bravery at Frederickstad earned him the DCM, but the award was, strangely enough, cancelled when his VC for Colenso was gazetted. The VC was presented to him by the Duke of Cornwall & York (later King George V) at Pietermaritzburg on August 14, 1901.

Due to the abject poverty he later lived in, his first three children were sent to foster homes in the USA and Canada.

Ravenhill's VC was forfeited on August 24, 1908, when he was convicted of theft of a vest. He was imprisoned for seven days as he couldn't pay the ten shilling fine that was imposed. It was one of eight VCs forfeited. The practice was discontinued in 1920 as King George V strongly disapproved of it. Ravenhill died at Birmingham on April 14, 1921, aged 49. He was interred at Witton Cemetery. His VC was sold by Sothebys in 1909 for £43. It is today in the Royal Scots Fusiliers Regimental Museum.

OD&M: VC, IGS, QSA (Relief of Ladysmith, Transvaal, Cape), KSA, Coronation Medal 1911.

MARTINEAU, Horace Robert, 25
Sergeant, Protectorate Regt, South African Forces

(Uys)

Born at Bayswater, London, on October 31, 1874, he was educated at the University College School. Martineau joined the XIth Hussars in September 1891, aged 16, and went to Natal with them the following year. He was garrisoned at Pietermaritzburg. From 1892-5 he served at Rawalpindi, India, then purchased his discharge and returned to South Africa to serve in the Matabele Rebellion of 1896 with Col Baden-Powell.

Martineau then served in the Cape Police and on outbreak of the Anglo-Boer War joined the Protectorate Regiment and served at the Defence of Mafeking. On Boxing Day, 1899, Baden-Powell launched an attack on the Boer positions on Game Tree Hill, two miles from the town's northern defences. The Boers expected the attack and had strengthened the fortifications.

Citation: On the 26th Dec 1899, during the fight at Game Tree, near Mafeking, when the order to retire had been given, Sergt Martineau stooped and picked up Corpl Le Camp, who had been struck down about ten yards from the Boer trenches, and half carried him towards a bush about 150 yards from the trenches. In doing this Sergt Martineau was wounded in the side, but paid no attention to it, and proceeded to staunch and bandage the wounds of his comrade, whom he afterwards assisted to retire. The firing while they were retiring was very heavy, and Sergt Martineau was again wounded. When shot the second time he was absolutely exhausted from supporting his comrade, and sank down, unable to proceed further. He received three wounds, one of which necessitated the amputation of his arm near the shoulder. (LG July 6, 1900).

Martineau saw no further fighting in the Anglo-Boer War and obtained employment in the government offices in Cape Town. He then served in the Bambata Rebellion of 1906. He worked for the African Boating Company, married Raymond Harman of Huelva, Spain, and had a daughter.

During World War I Lieut Martineau served in the Transport Service of the ANZACS at Suez and Gallipoli. He became ill with fever and was invalided to New Zealand, where he died at Dunedin on April 8, 1916, aged 41. He is buried in the Anderson's Bay Cemetery, Dunedin. In 1933 his daughter, Daphne, married a Royal Navy officer.

OD&M: VC, BSA Coy Medal (Clasp Rhodesia 1896), QSA (Def of Mafeking, OFS, Tvl), KSA, Natal 1906, 1914-15 Star, BWM, AVM, Coronation Medal 1911.

RAMSDEN, Horace Edward, 21
Trooper, Protectorate Regiment, South African Forces

A descendant of Sir John Ramsden, he was born at Chester, England, on December 15, 1878. His family immigrated to South Africa in 1891 and he and his younger brother, Alfred, attended school in Cape Town. At age 17 Ramsden joined Prince Alfred's Own Cape Artillery and served in the Bechuanaland Rebellion.

(Sotheby's)

On outbreak of the Anglo-Boer War he joined the Protectorate Regt and reluctantly smuggled Alfred onto the train to serve with him in Mafeking. They were in the abortive attack on Game Tree Hill on Boxing Day.

Citation: On the 26ᵗʰ Dec 1899, during the fight at Game Tree, near Mafeking, after the order to retire was given, Trooper H E Ramsden picked up his brother, Trooper A E Ramsden, who had been shot through both legs and was lying about ten yards from the Boer trenches, and carried him about 600 or 800 yards under heavy fire (putting him down from time to time to rest), till they met some men who helped to carry him to a place of safety. (London Gazette, July 6, 1900).

In Oct 1900 Horace received his VC from Lord Roberts in Pretoria. It was the second VC awarded to a soldier for saving his brother's life. The first was to Sir CJS Gough. Ramsden was fêted in Woodstock, Cape Town, then promoted lieutenant and transferred to Lord Roberts's Bodyguard.

After the war he obtained a commission in the Johannesburg Mounted Rifles, married a widow, Ada Tomlinson, and had a son. During World War I he served with Hartigan's Horse in South West Africa where he was taken prisoner by the Germans. He later divorced and in 1934 remarried Mary Levy. Ramsden died at Wynberg, Cape, on Aug 3, 1948, and was cremated.

Alfred's leg was amputated. He married Nurse Gertrude Aston and had three sons. He worked at De Beers in Somerset West, where he died in 1935. His medal with Horace's group were sold in October 1999 for £52,000.

OD&M: VC, CGS (Bar Bechuanaland), QSA (Bars Defence of Mafeking, OFS, Tvl, SA01, SA02), KSA (SA01, SA02), 1914-15 Star, BWM, Bilingual AVM, SA Police Good Service Medal, Coronation Medals 1911 and 1937.

(With the Flag)

The attack on Game Tree Fort.

29

1900

MILBANKE, Sir John Peniston, 27, Bart
Lieut (Tenth Baronet), 10th Hussars

Born in London on October 9, 1872, he was educated at Dover and Harrow. He joined the 10th Hussars in Nov 1892. Milbanke succeeded his father in Nov 1899. During the western campaign in South Africa he served as ADC to General French. While near Colesberg Sir John Milbanke wished to reconnoitre a hill and took a corporal and three men with him.

(Creagh)

Citation: On the 5th Jan 1900, during a reconnaissance near Colesberg, Sir John Milbanke when retiring under fire with a small patrol of the 10th Hussars, notwithstanding the fact that he had been severely wounded in the thigh, rode back to the assistance of one of the men whose pony was exhausted, and who was under fire from some Boers who had dismounted. Sir John Milbanke took the man up on his own horse under a most galling fire, and brought him safely back to camp. (LG July 6, 1900).

Sir John was promoted captain and awarded the Victoria Cross by the Queen in Dec 1900. He was the first Baronet to be gazetted the VC and one of the first five recipients to be decorated for the war.

His investiture was unique in that it took place during his honeymoon. On Dec 6, 1900, Sir John married Leila, only daughter of Col the Hon Charles Crichton, and had two sons. The couple then sailed to South Africa, where Sir John took up an administrative post under Lord Kitchener.

A picture of him in uniform appeared in the 'Black & White Budget' (Vol 3 p 750) of Sep 15, 1900   He retired from the army in 1910, but rejoined in 1914. He was appointed lieut-colonel of the Nottinghamshire Yeomanry (Sherwood Foresters) and served in the Dardanelles.

On Aug 21, 1915, he led a charge on the Turks holding Burnt Hill (Hill 70) at Gallipoli. According to the 'Globe' of Sep 4, 1915, "The Yeomanry moved forward in a solid mass, forming up under the lower western and northern slopes. It was now almost dark and the attack seemed to hang in the air, when suddenly the Yeomanry leapt to their feet, and as a single man charged right up the hill.

"They were met by a withering fire, which rose to a crescendo as they neared the northern crest, but nothing could stop them. They charged at amazing speed without a single halt from the bottom to the top, losing many men and

A Victoria Cross incident - Sir John Milbanke.

31

many of their chosen leaders, including gallant Sir John Milbanke..."

Sir John was killed when aged 43 years and is commemorated on the Helles Memorial at Gallipoli. Lady Milbanke later married Lieut-Gen Sir Bryan Mahon KCB DSO. A son, Wing Commander Sir John Milbanke, died in 1947 to be succeeded by his bachelor brother, Ralph. The latter served with the Royal Armoured Corps (Hussars) in 1940 and won the MC. He contracted enteritis and committed suicide in Nov 1949.

OD&M.: VC, QSA (Six clasps), 1914-15 Star, BWM, AVM, Coronation Medals 1911 and 1937.

DIGBY JONES, Robert James, 23
Royal Engineers

(Creagh)

Born at Edinburgh on Sept 27, 1876, he was educated in Northumberland, then Yorkshire.   An all-round athlete, he excelled at football and cricket.   Digby Jones went to Woolwich in 1894 and was commissioned two years later.

His relatives included famous military personalities such as a grand-uncle (Major-Gen Christie of the Afghan War) and two cousins involved in the Indian Mutiny (Major-Gen Graham and Lieut-Col Aitken VC, the defender of the Guard Gate at Lucknow).

Digby-Jones was posted to the 23rd Coy, Royal Engineers, promoted lieutenant and in June 1899 proceeded with them to Ladysmith, Natal. He was initially employed in the construction of a hospital and on the defences of the town.

Lieut Digby Jones was responsible on Dec 10/11 for blowing up an enemy 4.7 inch howitzer on Surprise Hill.   The first fuse inserted was defective and he went back, at the risk of his life, to insert another.

From 6.30 pm on Jan 5, 1900, he was in charge of 33 NCO's and men who were detailed to work that night on the Wagon Hill defences.   The southern perimeter defences of Ladysmith was on a hill which had Caesar's Camp in the east and Wagon Point in the west.

They were attacked early the following morning and Digby Jones took command until the arrival of Major Miller-Wallnutt. The Boers attacked the hill from Caesar's Camp in the east to Wagon Point in the west. Among the ILH troopers in support in the west was Herman Albrecht, 23.

Citation: Robert James Thomas Digby Jones, Royal Engineers; H Albrecht, No 459, Trooper, Imperial Light Horse. Would have been recommended for the Victoria Cross had they survived, on account of their having during the attack on Wagon Hill (Ladysmith), on 6 Jan 1900, displayed conspicuous bravery and gallant conduct in leading the force which reoccupied the top of

Lieutenant Digby-Jones' bravery at Wagon Hill.

the hill at a critical moment just as the three foremost attacking Boers reached it, the leader being shot by Lieut Jones and the two others by Albrecht. (LG August 8, 1902: Confirmation of V.C. awards).

At the time Digby Jones said, "What's up? The infantry have gone." Someone answered, "There is an order to retire, sir." Digby Jones said, "I have no order to retire." He ordered the men to fix bayonets and reoccupy the firing line. Later while leading his men forward he was shot in the throat and killed.

On the day that he was killed Digby Jones's younger brother received his commission in the Royal Engineers. His medal was given to his family in accordance with the regulations of Aug 8, 1902, which sanctioned posthumous awards. A cairn was erected on the spot where he fell by the Sappers, a brass tablet put up in St Mary's Cathedral, Edinburgh by his parents and brothers, and another in the Parish Church at Alnmouth by former Scottish schoolfriends.

OD&M: VC, QSA (Defence of Ladysmith).

ALBRECHT, Herman, 23
Trooper, Imperial Light Horse, South African Forces

Born in 1876 he was orphaned while young and was brought up in the Burghersdorp - Aliwal North area of the Northern Cape by Mr P Shorten. An excellent sportsman he made money by driving a postcart and breaking in horses. On outbreak of the war he joined the Imperial Light Horse as a trooper and was invested in Ladysmith. Albrecht was at Wagon Point at the critical time when the Boers raced toward the sangars.

(Uys)

Citation: See R J T Digby Jones Citation (LG August 8, 1902: Confirmation of VC awards).

At the gun pits Field Cornet De Villiers shot Major Miller-Wallnut through the head. He was shot by Albrecht, who a moment later was shot by Field Cornet De Jager, who in turn was killed by Lieut Digby Jones.

Albrecht was buried in a communal grave with other ILH dead at Wagon Hill. His VC was acquired by the SA National Museum of Military History in Johannesburg.

OD&M: VC, QSA (Elandslaagte, Defence of Ladysmith).

MASTERSON, James Edward Ignatius, 37
Lieut, 1st Bn, The Devonshire Regt

He was born on June 20, 1862. Masterson joined the
87th Royal Irish Fusiliers in 1881 and served in Egypt
the following year. In 1891 he was commissioned in
the 2nd Devonshire Regt, then served in Burma and on
the North-West Frontier of India.

(Wilkins)

During the Anglo-Boer War he was present at
Elandslaagte, Rietfontein and Lombard's Kop,
Ladysmith. He commanded D Company of the
Devons at Wagon Hill during their charge of the Boer positions at 6 pm.

Citation: During the action at Wagon Hill, on the 6th Jan 1900, Lieut.
Masterson commanded, with the greatest gallantry and dash, one of the three
companies of his regiment which charged a ridge held by the enemy, and
captured their position. The companies were then exposed to a most heavy
and galling fire from the right and left front. Lieut Masterson undertook to
give a message to the Imperial Light Horse, who were holding a ridge some
hundred yards behind, to fire to the left front and endeavour to check the
enemy's fire. In taking this message he crossed an open space of a hundred
yards which was swept by a most heavy cross-fire, and, although badly
wounded in both thighs, managed to crawl in and deliver his message before
falling exhausted into the Imperial Light Horse trench. His unselfish heroism
was undoubtedly the means of saving lives. (LG June 4, 1901).

According to the Times History, "Firing to the last second the Boers turned and
ran. But at the first convenient rocks they halted, still grimly determined not to
be hunted down the hill in daylight. For the next half hour the fight went on,
the Devons losing almost as heavily as in the charge. It was now that [Lieut]
Field and [Capt] Lafone were killed, and Masterson wounded in half a dozen
places while most gallantly carrying back a message for supports. A few
minutes later it was dark, and the Boers now finally abandoned the hill ..."

Masterson was promoted captain in 1900. In 1911 he was promoted major in
the King's Own Loyal Lancashire Regt and the following year retired. In 1910
he re-enacted at an army pageant the capture of the first French Eagle during
the Peninsular War by his ancestor, Sgt Patrick Masterson of the 87th. He

served as a Transport Officer from 1914-15. Masterson died at Waterlooville, Hampshire, on December 24, 1935. A tablet was placed in Exeter Cathedral in his memory.

OD&M: VC, Egypt 1882 (Bar Tel el Kebir), Khedive's Star, Burma Medal and clasp, India Medal (Two clasps), QSA (Elandslaagte and Defence of Ladysmith), 1914-15 Star, BWM, AVM, Coronation Medal 1911.

The charge of the Devons.

(With the Flag)

SCOTT, Robert, 25
Private, 1ˢᵗ Bn, The Manchester Regt

He was born in Haslingden, Lancashire, on June 4,
1874. Scott joined the Manchester Regt in Feb 1895
and was serving with them in Natal when the war
began. Scott was under the command of Lieut R
Hunt-Grubbe when they were attacked at Caesar's
Camp, east of Wagon Hill.

(Wilkins)

Citation: R Scott, Private and J Pitts, Private, 1ˢᵗ Bn,
The Manchester Regiment. During the attack on Caesar's Camp, in Natal, on
the 6ᵗʰ Jan 1900, these two men occupied a sangar, on the left of which all men
had been shot down and their positions occupied by Boers, and held their post
for fifteen hours without food or water, all the time under an extremely heavy
fire, keeping up their fire and a smart look-out, though the Boers occupied
some sangars on their immediate left rear. Private Scott was wounded. (LG
July 26, 1901).

By the end of the day only these two men survived at a post that had been held
by 16 men. Robert Scott later became a quartermaster-sergeant. He died at
Downpatrick, Co Down, Ireland, on February 22, 1961, aged 84 years.

OD&M: VC, QSA (Defence of Ladysmith), Coronation Medals 1911, 1937
and 1953.

PITTS, James, 22
Private, 1ˢᵗ Bn, The Manchester Regiment

James Pitts was born at Blackburn, Lancashire, on
Feb 26, 1877. He enlisted in the Manchester Regt and
at the age of 22 found himself involved in the Defence
of Ladysmith.

Citation: See Private R Scott (LG July 26, 1901).

(The Register)

Pitts was promoted lance-corporal and was decorated
with the VC by Lord Kitchener at Pretoria in June 1902. He later served in the
Army Reserve. While he was unemployed in 1908 he was approached to sell

his VC and indignantly refused, saying that he would rather suffer than part with it.

For the next 34 years Pitts worked as a roadman with the Blackburn Corporation. He married three times and was widowed finally in 1952. He died at Blackburn on Feb 18, 1955, aged 78. There is a monument, showing Pvt Pitts standing over the wounded Pvt Scott, in St Anne's Square, Manchester.

OD&M: VC, QSA (Defence of Ladysmith), Coronation Medals 1911, 1937 and 1953.

PARSONS, Francis Newton, 24
Lieut, The Essex Regt

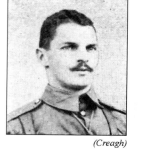

Born on March 23, 1875, at Dover, he was the third son of Dr Charles Parsons. Parsons was educated at Dover College and at Cambridge and Sandhurst. He joined the 1st Bn Essex Regt in Feb 1896 and was promoted lieutenant in March 1898. He accompanied his regiment to South Africa.

(Creagh)

After the Relief of Kimberley by Gen French's cavalry on February 15 Gen Cronje was forced to abandon his position at Magersfontein. He intended moving along the Modder River to Bloemfontein, but was slowed down by his ox-wagons, which gave French the chance to block his way at Koedoesrand. The Boers then formed a laager near Paardeberg, on the Modder River, and repulsed all attacks the British made on them.

The Essex Regt were involved in an action at Kitchener's Kopje, south-east of Cronje's laager, on February 18. According to the Times History, "Meanwhile the 81st Battery was in serious danger. Receiving an order to retire, it had begun limbering up when it immediately came under a tremendous rifle and pom-pom fire, which killed most of the horses.

"An attempt to rush the battery was frustrated by a party of the Essex under Lieutenant Parsons, who displayed exceptional gallantry and promptitude on this occasion, and by a number of odds and ends of other units which Capt Maurice hurriedly collected."

Citation: On the morning of the 18th Feb 1900, at Paardeberg, on the south bank of the Modder River, Private Ferguson 1st Battn Essex Regt, was wounded and fell in a place devoid of cover. While trying to crawl under cover, he was again wounded, in the stomach. Lieut Parsons at once went to his assistance, dressed his wound, under heavy fire, went down twice (still under heavy fire) to the bank of the river to get water for Private Ferguson, and subsequently carried him to a place of safety. This officer was recommended for the Victoria Cross by Lieut-General Kelly-Kenny, CB, on the 3rd March last. Lieutenant Parsons was killed on the 10th March, in the engagement at Driefontein, on which occasion he again displayed conspicuous gallantry. (LG Nov 20, 1900).

Francis Parsons is buried on the farm Bosrand in the Jacobsdal district. A memorial tablet was erected at Driefontein (west of Bloemfontein and south of Abraham's Kraal) to him, seven other officers, one warrant officer and 189 NCO's and men of the Essex Regt who died in the war. It was unveiled by Gen Sir Evelyn Wood in 1903.
 His medals were presented to the Regimental Museum at Warley, Essex, by his family in 1962. His name is also commemorated on the St Mary's Church war memorial at Dover.

OD&M: VC, QSA (Relief of Kimberley, Paardeberg, Driefontein).

ATKINSON, Alfred, 26
Sergeant, 1st Bn, The Yorkshire Regt

He was born at Armley, Leeds on Feb 6, 1874. His father, Farrier-Major James Atkinson, H Battery, 4th Brigade, RA, served in the Crimea and was said to have been one of the party which captured the cannon from which the VC's were later cast. Atkinson joined the Yorkshire Regt then went on the Reserve. He rejoined the Colours from the Reserve on outbreak of the South African War.

(Wilkins)

Citation: During the Battle of Paardeberg, 18 Feb, 1900, Sergt A Atkinson, 1st Bn, Yorkshire Regt, went out seven times, under heavy and close fire, to obtain water for the wounded. At the seventh attempt he was wounded in the head, and died a few days afterwards. (LG Aug 8, 1902).

Alfred Atkinson is buried in the Gruisbank Garden of Remembrance at

Paardeberg. He was the first Leeds man to win the VC. In 1911 his medals and his father's Crimean medals were sold to Mr Spink for £70. They are now in the regimental museum.

OD&M: VC, QSA (Relief of Kimberley, Paardeberg).

CURTIS, Albert Edward, 34.
Private, 2nd Bn, The East Surrey Regt

(Wilkins)

He was born at Guildford, Surrey, on Jan 6, 1866. Curtis joined the East Surrey Regt and took part in the final breakthrough by Buller at the Tugela, when the right flank took the Monte Christo Hill then crosssed the Tugela and assaulted the heights.

On February 23 Private Curtis took part in the Surrey Regiment's charge at Wynne's Hill (Onderbank Spruit). According to Curtis, "At daybreak the next morning [23rd] some got the order to retire but part of the hill that my section and all of A Company were on got the order to advance, so off we went at the double with our rifles at the slope. Just as we rose from our cover the Boers put on a most deadly fire. You could see nothing but men being knocked over. Then someone gave the order to get under cover, so we dropped down where we were and crept behind any stone that was near us.

"All day some of our chaps tried to get away but every time they rose they would go a few yards and then be knocked over. I saw Lieut Hinton [aged 26] go to where I knew the colonel [Harris of the East Surreys] was laying. He had know [no] sooner got to him than he was shot dead. I did not know that the colonel was wounded at this time but about four in the afternoon I heard groaning in the direction of where the colonel was laying. I came to the conclusion that he was wounded so I rose up from my cover and made for the colonel but had to get under cover again as the fire became too heavy and the way I got to him was to dodge from stone to stone until I reached him. I asked him if he was hurt and he said, 'I'm hit all over the body' but he said, 'Who are you?'` and I said, 'One of your own regiment' come to try and get you away'...

Citation: On the 23 February 1900, Colonel Harris lay all day long in a perfectly open space under close fire of a Boer Breastwork. The Boers fired all day at any man who moved and Colonel Harris was wounded eight or nine times. Private Curtis, after several attempts, succeeded in reaching the

Colonel, bound his wounded arm, and gave him his flask all under heavy fire. He then tried to carry him away, but was unable, on which he called for assistance and Private Morton came out at once. Fearing that the men would be killed, Colonel Harris told them to leave him, but they declined, and after trying to carry the Colonel on their rifles, they made a chair with their hands and so carried him out of the fire. (LG Jan 15, 1901).

After carrying Col Harris to safety, Privates Curtis and Morton, an old soldier, left him to find a stretcher. The colonel had incurred ten separate wounds. Meanwhile Privates Diamond and Connor arrived with a stretcher and carried him off. It was months later that Col Harris's replacement found out who had originally rescued him.

Curtis was awarded the VC and Private T W Morton the DCM. Curtis was promoted corporal, later sergeant, and decorated with the VC at Pietermaritzburg by the Duke of York (Later King George V) in Aug 1901. He became a Yeoman Warder at the Tower of London in 1910.

In 1914 Sergt Curtis trained recruits at the East Surrey Depot. He said to Private Cator, "Well, my boy, you must try and beat me." His pupil did, earning the VC, MM and Croix de Guerre. Curtis retired as a 'Beefeater' in 1931 and died at Barnet, Hertfordshire, on March 28, 1940. His medals were sold by Spinks in October 1999 for £40,000.

OD&M: VC, QSA. (Tugela Hts, OFS, Relief of Ladysmith, Transvaal, Laings Nek), KSA (SA01 and SA02), Coronation Medals 1911 and 1937.

INKSON, Edgar Thomas, 27
Lieut, Royal Army Medical Corps

The son of Surgeon-General J Inkson, he was born at Naini Tal, India on April 5, 1872. He studied at Edinburgh and London to qualify as a surgeon, then joined the Army Medical Corps in 1899. Lieut Inkson proceeded to South Africa as Medical Officer of the 7th, 14th and 66th Batteries, RFA.

(Wilkins)

He was with these batteries when the guns were lost at Colenso, and was then transferred to the 27th Royal Inniskilling Fusiliers (Hart's Brigade). Inkson served with them at Spion Kop and Vaal Krantz before being in action on the Tugela Heights.

Citation: Edgar Thomas Inkson, Lieut, Royal Army Medical Corps. On the 24th Feb 1900, Lieut Inkson carried 2nd Lieut Devenish (who was severely wounded and unable to walk) for three or four hundred yards, under a very heavy fire, to a place of safety. The ground over which Lieut Inkson had to move was much exposed, there being no cover available. (LG Jan 15, 1901).

Inkson rejoined the artillery batteries after the relief of Ladysmith, serving with Hunter's division then with Ian Hamilton's column. He rejoined the Inniskilling Fusiliers in April 1901 and served with them for the remainder of the war, part of the time with Allenby's column. In 1904 he married Ethel Bromley and they had a son and a daughter.

During the European War Lieut-Col Inkson commanded No 2 Field Hospital, 1st Division. He was awarded the DSO in January 1917, when he assumed command of No 1 General Hospital. In Aug 1917 he was given command of No 4 Stationary Hospital.

Colonel Inkson's army service included three years at Constantinople, four years as deputy director of medical services, Gibraltar, and 11 years as medical officer to the Royal Sussex Regiment at Chichester Barracks.

Colonel Inkson died at Chichester, Sussex, on February 19, 1947, aged 74, and was cremated at Woking, Surrey, and his ashes buried at Brookwood Cemetery. His only son served as a major in the South Staffordshire Regiment and in 1951 married Valerie Laman of Holland.

OD&M: VC, DSO, QSA (Five clasps), KSA (SA01, SA02), 1914-15 Star, BWM, AVM, Coronation Medals 1911 and 1937.

FIRTH, James, 26
Sergeant, 1st Bn, Duke of Wellington's (West Riding) Regt

(Spinks)

Born at Sheffield on Jan 15, 1874, he was educated near Newcastle-on-Tyne and joined the army in July 1889, aged 15. In June 1897 Firth married Mary Edwards. He was promoted sergeant and sent to the Cape with his unit. On February 22, 1900, Sergeant Firth brought natives out of a farm, who were required for intelligence purposes, under a severe cross-fire. Two days later he won the VC six miles north-west of Arundel (between Colesberg and Noupoort).

Citation: During the action at Plewman's Farm, near Arundel, Cape Colony, on 24 February 1900, Lance-Corporal Blackman having been wounded and lying exposed to a hot fire at the range of from 400-500 yards, Sergeant Firth picked him up and carried him to cover. Later in the day, when the enemy had advanced to within a short distance of the firing line, 2nd Lieutenant Wilson being dangerously wounded and in a most exposed position, Sergeant Firth carried him over the crest of the ridge, which was being held by the troops, to shelter, and was himself shot through the nose and eye whilst doing so. (LG June 11, 1901).

He was first wrongly gazetted as W Firth. The Firths had two children, Alleyne born in 1903 and Cecil in 1907. He wore an eye-patch for the rest of his life. Firth died at Sheffield, Yorkshire, on May 29, 1921, and is buried in the Burngreave Cemetery. Spinks sold his medals in October 1999 for £38,000.

OD&M: VC, QSA (Cape Colony), Coronation Medal 1911.

MANSEL-JONES, Conwyn, 28
Captain, West Yorkshire Regt

(Wilkins)

Born at Beddington, Surrey, on June 14, 1871, the son of a judge, he was educated at Haileybury and Sandhurst. Mansel-Jones was commissioned in the Prince of Wales's Own West Yorkshire Regt in Oct 1890. He served in the Ashanti Expedition of 1895-6 and in British Central Africa 1898-9. He was promoted captain in March 1899.

On outbreak of the Anglo-Boer War Jones rejoined his regiment in Natal. During the fight for the Tugela Heights, according to the Times History, "As the West Yorks, now joined by some of the South Lancashires, pushed across the summit they met with a heavy fire from the far side (For rallying some of the men on this occasion Captain Mansel Jones received the Victoria Cross). But they were not to be stopped and swept right over the top, capturing a maxim and several prisoners. Then manning the Boer sangars they poured a heavy fire after their retreating enemies (5 pm)..."

Citation: On the 27th Feb 1900, during the assault on Terrace Hill, north of the Tugela, in Natal, the companies of the West Yorkshire Regt on the northern slope of the hill met with a severe shell, Vickers-Maxim and rifle fire, and their advance was for a few minutes checked. Captain C Mansel-Jones, however, by his strong initiative, restored confidence, and in spite of his falling very seriously wounded, the men took the whole ridge without further check; this officer's self-sacrificing devotion to duty at a critical moment having averted what might have proved a serious check to the whole assault. (LG July 27, 1900).

Mansel-Jones's leg was amputated. He was DAAG for Recruiting from 1901 to 1910, then retired due to ill-health caused by his war wounds. In 1913 he married Marion Barton-Wright and the following year was called to the Bar. On outbreak of World War I he went to France as DAAG at General Headquarters. He was created a Companion of the DSO in June 1915.

   In 1917 Lieut-Col Mansel-Jones was created Officier de la Legion d'Honneur by the French president and in 1918 was awarded the CMG. From 1920-42 he was a member of the Hon Corps of the Gentleman-at-Arms. He died at Lymington, Brockenhurst, Hampshire, on May 29, 1942, aged 70, and is buried at St Nicholas Churchyard, Brockenhurst.

OD&M: VC, CMG, DSO, QSA (Relief of Ladysmith, Tugela Heights), 1914-15 Star, BWM, AVM, Coronation Medals 1911 and 1937.

ENGLEHEART, Henry William, 36
Sergeant, 10th Royal Hussars (The Prince of Wales's Own)

Born at Blackheath, Kent, on Nov 14, 1863, he was the son of a stockbroker and grandson of the last of the Queen's Proctors.

(Wilkins)

Citation: [On March 13, 1900] He was one of the party, under Brevet Major Aylmer Hunter Weston, that successfully destroyed the railway north of Bloemfontein. They had to charge through a Boer Piquet, besides getting over four deep spruits, in order to creep back through the Boer lines. At the last of these spruits Sapper Webb's horse fell, and consequently he was left in a very dangerous position. Sergt Engleheart went back to his assistance, through a deadly storm of shot and shell. He had to lose some time in getting Webb and his horse out of the spruit, and every moment the position became worse, owing to the rapid advance of the Boers. At last he succeeded in getting Webb back to the party. Just before this Sergt Engelbrecht had shown great gallantry in dashing into the first spruit, which could only be approached in single file, and was still held by a party of Boers. (LG Oct 5, 1900).

The VC was presented to him on Dec 15, 1900, shortly before Queen Victoria died. Sergeant Engleheart was the centre man of the last five to receive it from the hands of the queen. He retired in 1908 while serving with his regiment in Rawalpindi, India. From then until 1936 he was a lodge keeper at Windsor Castle.

Engelheart died at Datchet, Berkshire, on August 9, 1939, and was cremated at Woking, Surrey. In 1978 his twin sons, Geoffrey and Hugh, presented his medals to the Royal Hussars at Winchester.

OD&M: VC, QSA, Coronation Medals 1911 amd 1937.

(With the Flag)

Winning a Victoria Cross near Bloemfontein.

PHIPPS-HORNBY, Edmund John, 42
Major, Q Battery, Royal Horse Artillery

Born on Dec 31, 1857, at Lordington, Emsworth, Hampshire, he was the second son of Admiral of the Fleet Sir Geoffrey Phipps-Hornby GCB. After his education at a private school and Woolwich he entered the RA in May 1878. He served in Warren's Bechuanaland Expedition of 1884-5 and was promoted captain the following year. In Jan 1895 Phipps-Hornby married Anna Jay of Bexley, Kent, and they had two daughters. That year he was promoted major.

(With the Flag)

After the surrender of Cronje at Paardeberg and the loss of Bloemfontein to Lord Roberts, Gen Christiaan de Wet let his men take leave. On their return he launched a surprise attack on Gen Broadwood's column at Koornspruit (Sannaspos) east of Bloemfontein. He concealed his men in a donga, which the column was crossing, and managed to kill or capture over 1,000 men.

Citation: Edmund John Phipps-Hornby, Major, Q Battery, Royal Horse Artillery. Date of Act of Bravery: 31 March 1900. On the occasion of the action at Korn Spruit on the 31st March, 1900, a British force, including two batteries of the Royal Horse Artillery, was retiring from Thabanchu, towards Bloemfontein. The enemy had formed an ambush at Korn Spruit, and, before their presence was discovered by the main body, had captured the greater portion of the baggage column and five out of the six guns of the leading battery. When the alarm was given, Q Battery, Royal Horse Artillery, was within three hundred yards of the spruit. Major Phipps-Hornby, who commanded it, at once wheeled about and moved off at a gallop under a very heavy fire. One gun was upset when the wheel horse was shot, and had to be abandoned with another waggon, the horses of which were killed. The remainder of the battery reached a position close to some unfinished railway buildings, and come into action 1,150 yards from the spruit, remaining in action until ordered to retire. When the order to retire was received, Major Phipps-Hornby ordered the guns and their limbers to be run back by hand to where the teams of uninjured horses stood behind the unfinished buildings. The few remaining gunners, assisted by a number of officers and men of a party of mounted infantry, and directed by Major Phipps-Hornby and Capt Humphreys, the only remaining officers of the battery, succeeded in running back four of the guns under shelter. One or two of the limbers were similarly withdrawn by hand, but the work was most severe and the distance considerable. In consequence, all concerned were so exhausted that they were unable to drag in the remaining limbers of the fifth gun. It now became necessary to risk the horses, and volunteers were called for from among the drivers, who readily responded. Several horses were killed and men wounded, but at length only one gun and one limber were left exposed. Four separate attempts were made to rescue these, but when no more horses were available the attempt had to be given up and the gun and limber were abandoned. Meanwhile the other guns had been sent on one at a time, and after passing within seven or eight hundred yards of the enemy, in rounding the head of a donga and crossing two spruits, they eventually reached a place of safety, where the battery was reformed. After full consideration of the circumstances of the case, the Field-Marshal Commanding-in-Chief in South Africa formed the opinion that the conduct of all ranks of 'Q' Battery, Royal Horse Artillery, was conspicuously gallant and daring, but that all were equally brave and devoted in their behaviour. He therefore decided to treat the case of the battery as one of collective gallantry, under Rule 13 of the Victoria Cross Warrant, and directed that one officer should be selected for the decoration of the Victoria Cross by the officers, one non-commissioned officer by the non-commissioned officers, and two gunners or drivers by the gunners and drivers. A difficulty arose with regard to the officer, owing to the fact that there were only two officers Major Phipps-Hornby and Capt Humphreys available for the work of saving the guns, and both of these had been conspicuous by their gallantry and by the fearless manner in which they exposed themselves, and each of them nominated the other for the decoration. It was ultimately decided in favour of Major Phipps-Hornby, as having been the senior concerned. Sgt C Parker was elected by the non-commissioned officers, as described above. Gunner I Lodge and Driver H H Glasock were elected by the gunners and drivers, as described above. (LG June 26, 1900).

Phipps-Hornby was decorated with the VC by Lord Roberts at Pretoria in Oct 1900. He was ADC to Lord Roberts from 1901-3, when he was promoted lieut-colonel. He was given command of the 4th RHA Brigade at Woolwich until 1908 when he was promoted colonel. From 1909-13 as a brigadier-general he commanded the 4th Division, during which time he was created a CB. His brother, meanwhile, had become an admiral of the Royal Navy.

On the outbreak of the World War Brig-Gen Phipps-Hornby commanded the Artillery III Corps in France. In 1916 he was created a CMG and commanded the artillery of the Southern Army in England until the end of the war, when he retired. General Phipps-Hornby died at Sonning-on-Thames, Berkshire, on December 13, 1947, 18 days short of his 90th birthday. His medals are in the Woolwich Mess of the Royal Artillery.

OD&M: VC, CB, CMG, QSA, 1914-15 Star, BWM, AVM, Coronation Medals 1911 and 1937.

The disaster at Koornspruit. The Royal Horse Artillery.

PARKER, Charles Edward Haydon, 30
Sergeant, Q Battery, Royal Horse Artillery

The son of a Crimean veteran he was born at Woolwich, on March 11, 1870. He entered the Royal Horse Artillery at the age of 15 and served in India from 1889-95, then in 1899 came to South Africa. He had two brothers serving in the same Battery RHA at the time.

(Creagh)

Citation: See Major Phipps-Hornby (LG June 26, 1900).

Parker enlisted in the RFA in 1914 and later became a Battery Sergeant-Major. He was affected by gas poisoning and influenza and died, aged 48 years, on Aug 9, 1918 at Coventry, Warwickshire. He is buried at London Road Cemetery, Coventry. Parker's medals were purchased from Glendinnings in 1963 by the RA for £720.

There is a Sergt C Parker VC, D Battery, RHA, buried at Stellawood Cemetery, Durban, who died on March 16, 1938, aged 77. One can only assume that this was an imposter.

OD&M: VC, QSA (Relief of Kimberley, Paardeberg, Driefontein, Diamond Hill, Wittebergen), 1914-15 Star, BWM, AVM, LSGC (Edward VII), Coronation Medal 1911.

LODGE, Isaac, 33
Gunner, Q Battery, Royal Horse Artillery

He was born at Great Canfield, Essex, on May 6, 1866, and attended school there. From the age of 11 Lodge worked on farms and as a gamekeeper. In Dec 1888 he joined the Royal Garrison Artillery and was transferred to the RHA for service in India. He came to South Africa with his battery in 1899.

(With the Flag)

Citation: See Major Phipps-Hornby (LG June 2, 1900).

He was presented with the VC by Lord Roberts in Pretoria in October 1900.

Lodge served with his battery in the Transvaal, then in the Cape where they were in action against Cmdt Scheepers. He later became a bombardier.

After 21 years service he retired from the army and became a Keeper at the Royal Parks, first at Regents Park, then Hyde Park. Among his medals the George V Coronation Medal was of the type awarded to Royal Park Keepers. His daughter, Gladys, 11, died in 1916.

Lodge died at Hyde Park, London, on June 13, 1923, aged 57. His medals were presented to the National Army Museum by his daughter-in-law, Mabel Parker.

OD&M: VC, QSA (Rel of Kimberley, Paarde, Drief, Tvl, SA01), Coronation Medal 1911, LSGC.

GLASOCK, Horace Henry, 19
Driver, Q Battery, Royal Horse Artillery

He was born at Islington, London, on October 16, 1880.

Citation: See Major Phipps-Hornby (LG June 26, 1900).

(With the Flag)

His name was initially incorrectly spelt as Glassock. He was decorated at Windsor Castle by Queen Victoria on Dec 15, 1900. He was discharged from the RHA in Jan 1911. He and his wife, Minnie, had three children and lived in Johannesburg. He joined the South African Defence Force and served in the Rebellion of 1914, then in South West Africa. Glasock served in East Africa in the SASC Animal Transport Unit, until found medically unfit due to malaria, dyspepsia and liver problems. He left with the rank of Conductor (Warrant Officer).

Glasock was invalided to Cape Town's Maitland General Hospital, but never recovered. He died on October 20, 1916, aged 36, and is buried in Grave 97317A in the military plot at Maitland Cemetery, Cape Town. His grave's headstone, which features a Springbok head, has recently been renewed.

OD&M: VC, QSA, 1914-15 Star, BWM, AVM, Coronation Medal 1911.

MAXWELL, Francis Aylmer, 28, DSO
Lieut, Indian Staff Corps (attached to Roberts's Light
Horse)

The son of a surgeon-major and the third of several
brothers, he was born on Sept 7, 1871, at Guildford,
Surrey. Maxwell joined the Indian Staff Corps in Dec
1893 and two years later served in Waziristan and
Chitral. From 1897-8 he was ADC to the GOC of the
Tirah Expeditionary Force, for which he was created a
Companion of the DSO.

(Wilkins)

    Lieutenant Maxwell's mounted swordsmanship and shooting were
exceptional. In 1899 he became adjutant of the Queen's Own Corps of Guides.
In Jan 1900 he volunteered to take remounts to South Africa and was not long
there when he became attached to Roberts' Light Horse.
    No Indian troops were employed in South Africa, other than as local
volunteers, who were employed as stretcher-bearers. Lieut Maxwell was the
only member of the Indian Army to win a VC during the Anglo-Boer War.
    Maxwell later told his mother, "My squadron was leading when about a
quarter of a mile from the stream an excited man galloped up and said the
Boers were right in the wagons disarming our men ... I galloped up to the
wagons and sure enough, without the smallest noise or confusion, were Boers
thick as peas, collecting arms from our men. There was no mistake, for I amost
rode one swine over ... Back I went, full split to the regiment, which had trotted
up to within 120 yards of the stream."
    Orders were given for the batteries to retire, but as they wheeled a wave of
bullets caught them. Men and horses went down. Maxwell and his loyal
Indian orderly, Dost Mohamed, refused to gallop and trotted to the shelter of
some tin buildings behind the gun line, giving a dismounted man a hand on the
way.
    He added, "Never was anything more magnificent than the way these men
fought. I wasn't 30 yards off and level with them and safe and sound behind the
tin hut, and from the very same an Australian and I ran out to help the colonel
commanding ... to drag a limber up to one of the guns so as to have the
ammunition nearer."

Citation: Lieut Maxwell was one of three officers, not belonging to Q Battery,
Royal Horse Artillery, specially mentioned by Lord Roberts as having shown
the greatest gallantry and disregard of danger in carrying out the sef-imposed
duty of saving the guns of that battery during the affair of Korn Spruit on the
31st March 1900. This officer went out on five different occasions, and
assisted to bring in two guns and three limbers, one of which he, Capt

Humphreys, and some gunners dragged in by hand. He also went out with Capt Humphreys and Lieut Stirling to try and get the last gun in, and remained there till the last gun was abandoned. During a previous campaign (the Chitral Expedition of 1895) Lieut Maxwell displayed gallantry in the removal of the body of Lieut-Colonel F D Battye, Corps of Guides, under fire, for which, though recommended, he received no reward. (LG March 6, 1901).

According to Wilkins, "This official statement of an act of gallantry in a previous campaign, included in the notification of that for which the cross is awarded in a later one, has not occurred before in the Victoria Cross records."

Maxwell was promoted captain in July 1901. The following month he was decorated with the VC by the Duke of Cornwall & York at Pietermaritzburg. Maxwell was then offered a post as ADC to Lord Kitchener. His outspokenness appealed to Kitchener, who dubbed him 'The Brat'. No two men understood each other better.

After the war he went to India with Lord Kitchener. In 1906 he married an Australian, Charlotte Osborne, and they had two daughters. From 1910-16 Major Maxwell was military secretary to the Governor General of India. In 1911 he was created a member of the Most Exalted Order of the Star of India (CSI).

During the First World War Maxwell commanded the 12th Bn, Middlesex Regt during the fight for Trones Wood, Somme, in July 1916 and was awarded a bar to his DSO. For his services in the taking of Thiepval he was promoted OC of the 18th Lancers, Indian Army in Oct 1916.

Brigadier-General Maxwell commanded the 27th Infantry Brigade, 9th Scottish Division, under the South African commander, General Lukin. He was among the most senior officers to meet his death at the front when he was shot by a sniper near Ypres on Sept 21, 1917. He is buried in the Ypres Reservoir Cemetery, Belgium. His medals were sold by Spinks in Nov 1998 for £78,000.

OD&M: VC, CSI, DSO and Bar, IGS 1854-95 (Clasp Waziristan), Chitral and Tirah), IGS 1895-1902 (Clasps Samana 1897, Relief of Chitral 1895, Punjab Frontier 1897-98, Tirah 1897-98) QSA (Clasps Cape, Paard, Drief, Jhbg, D Hill, Witt), KSA (SA01, SA02), 1914-15 Star, BWM, AVM (MID), Coronation Medals 1902 and 1911, Delhi Durbar 1911.

NICKERSON, William Henry Snyder, 25
Lieut, Royal Army Medical Corps

Born at New Brunswick, Canada, on March 27, 1875,
he was the son of a chaplain to HM's Forces.
Nickerson was educated at Portsmouth, qualified as a
doctor at Manchester University and joined the
RAMC in July 1898. He was attached to the Mounted
Infantry in South Africa and served with Gen Buller's
field force which invaded the Transvaal from Natal.

(Wilkins)

Citation: At Wakkerstroom on the evening of the 20th April 1900, during the
advance of the infantry to support the mounted troops, Lieut Nickerson went in
a most gallant manner, under a heavy shell and rifle fire, to attend a wounded
man, dressed his wounds, and remained with him until he had him conveyed to
a place of safety. (LG Feb 12, 1901).

For his distinguished service Nickerson was promoted captain in Nov 1900.
He served in West Africa and Ireland and was promoted major in July 1909.
Nickerson served with the cavalry during the 1914 retreat in France, 1st and 2nd
Ypres, Neuve Chapelle and from Dec 1915 in Salonika. Lieut-Colonel
Nickerson was created a CMG in 1916. He married Nan Waller in 1918 and
they had a son and a daughter.

He was promoted major-general and from 1925-33 was honorary surgeon to
the king and colonel commandant of the RAMC until 1945. During this time
he served on an Atlantic convoy, the Port of London Emergency Service and
the Home Guard. He died at Cour, Kintyre, Scotland on April 10, 1954, aged
79 years, and is buried there in the family's vault.

OD&M: VC, CB, CMG, QSA (Cape, OFS, Tvl), KSA (SA01, SA02), 1914
Star (Mons clasp), BWM, AVM, Coronation Medals 1911, 1937 and 1953.

BEET, Harry Churchill, 27
Corporal, 1st Bn, Derbyshire Regiment

He was born near Bingham, Notts, on April 1, 1873. Beet joined the Derbyshire Regt (Sherwood Foresters) in Feb 1892. Two years later he sailed to India and fought on the Indian Punjab Frontier from 1897-8. The following year he came to South Africa and served with the 2nd Mounted Infantry Company.

(Wilkins)

Citation: At Wakkerstroom on the 22nd April, 1900, No 2 Mounted Infantry Company, 1st Bn Derbyshire Regt, with two squadrons of Imperial Yeomanry, had to retire from near a farm, under a ridge held by Boers, Corporal Burnett, Imperial Yeomanry, was left on the ground wounded, and Cpl Beet, on seeing him, remained behind and placed him under cover, bound up his wounds, and by firing prevented the Boers from coming down to the farm till dark, when Dr Wilson, Imperial Yeomanry, came to the wounded man's assistance. The retirement was carried out under a very heavy fire, and Cpl Beet was exposed to fire during the whole afternoon. (LG Feb 12, 1901).

Beet was promoted sergeant by Lord Kitchener for his services. He was wounded near Virginia on Dec 9, 1901. Early in 1916 he was commissioned in the 32nd Reserve Canadian Infantry Battalion. He died at Rupert, Vancouver, Canada on Jan 10, 1946, aged 72 years. Beet's medals were purchased by his regiment for £2,800 in 1973, and they are displayed at Nottingham Castle.

OD&M: VC, India Medal (Punjab Frontier 1897-8, Tirah 1897-8), QSA (Cape, OFS. Tvl), KSA (SA01, SA02), BWM, AVM, Coronation Medal 1937.

MACKAY, John Frederick, 26
Lance-Corporal, 1st Bn, The Gordon Highlanders

Born at Edinburgh on June 6, 1873, he was a university student before joining the 1st Bn Gordon Highlanders. He saw service on the North-West Frontier of India and in the Tirah Expedition of 1897-8. In South Africa he was present at Magersfontein and Paardeberg, then in the advance on Johannesburg fought close to where the Jameson Raiders had been

(Creagh)

captured in 1895, south-west of the city.

Citation: On the 20th May 1900, during the action at Doornkop near Johannesburg, MacKay repeatedley rushed forward, under a withering fire at short range, to attend to wounded comrades, dressing their wounds whilst himself was without shelter, and in one instance carrying a wounded man from the open under heavy fire to the shelter of a boulder. (LG Aug 10, 1900).

Mackay saw further service at Pretoria, Belfast and the Eastern Transvaal. On July 11, 1900, he fought at Wolvekrantz, near Krugersdorp, and was again recommended for the VC. He was transferred to the King's Own Scottish Borderers for the duration of the war.
   He was decorated by Lord Roberts at Pretoria on Oct 25, 1900. From 1903 he served with the Southern Nigeria Regt, then in 1907 transferred to the Argyll and Sutherland Highlanders. Lieut-Colonel Mackay served in France in 1915-6, then commanded the 2/6th Bn Highland Light Infantry, until its disbandment.
   He suffered from the effects of his wounds and went to Nice, France, in Oct 1929 for treatment, but died there on Jan 9, 1930, aged 56.

OD&M: VC, India Medal (Tirah 1897-8), QSA (Five clasps), KSA (SA01, SA02), West Africa GSM (Four clasps), 1914-15 Star, BWM, AVM (MID).

KIRBY, Frank Howard, 28, DCM
Corporal, Royal Engineers

(Creagh)

Born at Thame, Oxfordshire, on Nov 12, 1871, he entered the Royal Engineers in London in Aug 1892. He was mobilised for South Africa in 1899. In March 1900 he blew up the Bloemfontein Railway line, for which he was awarded the DCM. He was meant to repeat this feat 'north of Kroonstad' while with Gen Hunter Weston's column.
   As Johannesburg was captured on May 31 and Pretoria on June 5, one can assume that Cpl Kirby was sent to sabotage the railway line from Pretoria to the eastern Transvaal. This turned out to be an abortive mission.

Citation: On the morning of the 2nd June 1900, a party sent to try to cut the

Delagoa Bay Railway were retiring, hotly pressed by very superior numbers. During one of the successive retirements of the rearguard, a man whose horse had been shot was running after his comrades. He was a long way behind the rest of his troop, and was under a brisk fire. From among the retiring troops Corpl Kirby turned and rode back to the man's assistance. Although by the time he reached him they were under a heavy fire at close range, Corpl Kirby managed to get the dismounted man up behind him and to take him clear off over the next ridge held by our reargaurd. This is the third occasion on which Corpl Kirby has displayed gallantry in the face of the enemy. (LG Oct 8, 1900).

Corporal Kirby was promoted Troop Sergeant-Major on the field by Lord Roberts in July 1900. Sergeant Kirby was decorated by the Duke of Cornwall & York at Cape Town on Aug 19, 1901.

He became a warrant officer in 1906 and three years later married Kate Jolly. They had two sons and two daughters. He was commissioned in April 1911 and the following year was gazetted to the Royal Flying Corps.

Kirby served in France in 1916-7 and was promoted captain in 1917 and later lieut-colonel. From 1918-26 he was a group captain in the RAF. He died at Sidcup, Kent, on July 8, 1956, aged 84 years. There is a tablet to his memory in the Chatham Garrison Church, Kent.

OD&M: VC, CBE, DCM, QSA (7 Clasps), 1914-15 Star, BWM, AVM (MID), LSGC (Edward VII), Coronation Medals 1911 and 1937.

WARD, Charles Burley, 22
Private, King's Own Yorkshire Light Infantry

He was born on July 10, 1877, at Hunslet, Leeds, Yorkshire. In April 1897 he enlisted in the Yorkshire Light Infantry and served in the Cape. He was serving under Major-General Paget in the OFS in June 1900, shortly after the towns on the route of advance had been garrisoned.

(Wilkins)

Citation: On the 26th June 1900, at Lindley, a picquet of the Yorkshire Light Infantry was surrounded on three sides by about 500 Boers at close quarters. The two officers were wounded, and all but six of the men were killed or wounded. Private Ward then volunteered to take a message asking for reinforcements to the signalling station, about 150 yards in the rear of the post. His offer was at first refused, owing to the practical certainty of his being shot; but on his insisting, he was allowed to go. He got across untouched through a storm of shots from each flank, and having delivered his message, he voluntarily retired from a place of absolute safety and re-crossed the fire-swept ground to assure his commanding officer that the message had been sent. On this occasion he was severely wounded. But for this gallant action the post would certainly have been captured. (LG Sep 28, 1900).

Due to his serious wound he saw little further action. He was the last winner of the VC to be decorated by Queen Victoria before her death. On his discharge the citizens of Leeds presented with a commemorative gold medal and £600. He served as an instructor during the 1914-18 War.

Ward died at the Glamorgan County Asylum, Wales, on Dec 30, 1921, aged 45 years. He is buried in St Mary's Churchyard, Whitchurch, Cardiff, and in 1986 the British Legion erected a headstone over his grave.

OD&M: VC, QSA (Cape, OFS), BWM, AVM, Coronation Medal 1911.

RICHARDSON, Arthur Herbert Lindsay, 27
Sergeant, Lord Strathcona's Horse, Canadian Forces

He was born at Southport, near Liverpool, Lancashire, on Sep 23, 1872. Richardson went to Canada in 1892 and worked as a dentist at Stoney Mountain, Manitoba, before joining the North-West Mounted Police in Regina in May 1894. Posted to Battleford, he was promoted corporal in 1898. He joined Lord Strathcona's Horse, a Canadian cavalry unit, and was present in the advance by Gen Buller into the Transvaal.

(Wilkins)

Citation: On the 5th July 1900, at Wolve Spruit, about fifteen miles north of Standerton, a party of Lord Strathcona's Corps, only thirty-eight in number, came into contact and was engaged at close quarters with a force of eighty of the enemy. When the order to retire had been given, Sergt Richardson rode back under a very heavy cross-fire and picked up a trooper whose horse had been shot and who was wounded in two places, and rode with him out of fire. At the time when this act of gallantry was performed Sergt Richardson was within 300 yards of the enemy, and was himself riding a wounded horse. (LG Sep 14, 1900).

Richardson was the first man to win a VC in a Canadian unit which was under a British command. As a token of their esteem his fellow Canadians presented him with a gift of £3,000. He was discharged in Ottawa in March 1901. Richardson returned to the 'Mounties', but performed poorly and purchased his discharge in Nov 1907.

Richardson became the Town Constable of Indian Head, Saskatchewan, but became debt ridden and pawned his medals. He returned to England in 1909 and worked in Liverpool. He was reunited with his family after an absence of 16 years. Known as the 'shy VC', he lived in obscurity and poverty.

He died at Liverpool on Dec 15, 1932, aged 59 years, and is buried in St James Cemetery.

OD&M: VC, QSA Medal is dated 1899-1900 (Natal, Belfast SA01), Coronation Medals 1902 and 1911.

GORDON, William Eagleson, 34
Captain, 1ˢᵗ Bn, The Gordon Highlanders

He was born at Bridge of Allan, Stirlingshire,
Scotland, on May 4, 1866, and joined the Gordon
Highlanders at Malta in June 1888. Lieutenant
Gordon served in the Chitral Relief Expedition of
1895. He was promoted captain in June 1897, then
served on the North-West Frontier and the Tirah
Expedition.

(Wilkins)

He was adjutant to the 1ˢᵗ Bn in South Africa and was
dangerously wounded at Magersfontein. Gordon was attended to on the
battlefield by Lieut Douglas, who earned the VC for so doing. He also served
at Paardeberg, operations in the OFS, Eastern Transvaal and west of Pretoria
from July 1900.

On 11 July 1900 Gen Smith-Dorrien left for the north from Krugersdorp with
the Gordons, Shropshires, two guns of the 78ᵗʰ Battery and half the 50th
Company Imperial Yeomanry. At Dwarsvlei, approximately nine miles (15
km) north-west of Krugersdorp on the Hekpoort road, they found Boers
holding a ridge, the Witwatersburg.

They were exposed to a deadly fire and, despite displaying great gallantry the
gunners were soon put out of action. Several attempts were made by the
Gordons to bring the guns back into cover. The force covered a front of 4,000
yards and was attacked on the right flank and right rear as well as in front.

Citation: On the 11ᵗʰ July 1900, during the action near Leehoehoek (or
Doornboschfontein, near Krugersdorp), a party of men, accompanied by
Captains Younger and Allan, having succeeded in dragging an artillery
waggon under cover when its horses were unable to do so by reason of the
heavy and accurate fire of the enemy, Capt Gordon called for volunteers to go
out with him to try and bring in one of the guns. He went out alone to the
nearest gun under a heavy fire, and with the greatest coolness fastened the
drag-rope to the gun, and then beckoned to the men, who immediately doubled
out to join him, in accordance with his previous instructions. While moving
the gun Capt Younger and three men were hit. Seeing that further attempts
would only result in further casualties, Capt Gordon ordered the remainder of
the party under cover of the kopje again, and, having seen the wounded safely
away, himself retired. Capt Gordon's conduct under a particularly heavy and
most accurate fire at only 600 yards' range was most admirable, and his
manner of handling his men most masterly; his devotion on every occasion
that his battalion has been under fire has been remarkable. (LG Sep 28, 1900).

Captain Gordon was presented with the VC by Lord Kitchener at Pretoria in June 1902. Gordon married and had a son. He was promoted major in January 1907. From April 1908 he was DAA and QMG of the Highland Division, and from 1913 ADC to the king. Colonel Gordon served in France until taken prisoner. He was released by exchange, then from Sep 1917-20 commanded No 1 (Midland) District, Scottish Command.

He was later awarded £500 damages after suing the 'People's Journal' for slander. They had erroneously reported him as ordering the Gordons to surrender when hard-pressed during the retreat from Mons.

During World War II Gordon was injured during an enemy air raid in Nov 1940. He and his wife were rescued from their bombed bedroom in London. As a result of his injuries he died at London on March 10, 1941, aged 74 years.

OD&M: VC, CBE, India Medal (Tirah 1897-8), QSA (Five clasps), KSA (SA01, SA02), 1914 Star (Mons clasp), BWM, AVM (MID), Coronation Medals, 1911 and 1937.

YOUNGER, David Reginald, 29
Captain, 1st Bn, The Gordon Highlanders

He was born at Edinburgh on March 17, 1871. Younger served in the Duke of Edinburgh's Edinburgh Artillery, then in Dec 1893 was commissioned in the Gordon Highlanders. He served on the Punjab Frontier from 1895-8, being present at the storming and capture of the Dargai Heights.

(Wilkins)

While serving in South Africa he showed extreme coolness under fire, especially at the Dwarsvlei Battle.

Citation: In recognition of the conspicuous bravery displayed by him on the same occasion (11 July 1900), would have been recommended to Her Majesty for the Victoria Cross had he survived. A later notice in the London Gazette of 8 Aug. 1902, read: "Date of Act of Bravery: 11 July 1900. This officer, during the action near Krugersdorp on the 11th July 1900 volunteered for and took out the party which successfully dragged a Royal Artillery wagon under cover of a small kopje, though exposed to a very heavy and accurate fire at only 850 yards' range. He also accompanied the second party of volunteers who went out to try and bring in one of the guns. During the afternoon he was mortally wounded, dying shortly afterwards. His cool and gallant conduct was the admiration of all who witnessed it, and, had Capt Younger lived, the Field-Marshal Commanding-in-Chief in South Africa would have recommended him for the high award of the Victoria Cross, at the same time as Capt W E Gordon, of the same regiment. (LG Sep 28, 1900 and Aug 8, 1902).

His place of death is given as Leehoehoek (Lion's Corner] and Doornboschfontein, Transvaal. Captain David Younger is buried in the Krugersdorp Garden of Remembrance, where his date of death is erroneously given as 11 June.

In 1984 a local, Owen Timmermans, found 16 schanzes on a ridge on the farm Weltevreden. His metal detector disclosed mauser and Martini-Henry cartridge casings, 15-pounder shells and shrapnel balls. A grandson of one of the Boer participants told him that only 23 Boers had fought there, "By spreading their positions and maintaining a fast rate of continuous firing they tricked the British into believing that they were surrounded by a superior force."

OD&M: VC, India Medal (Three clasps), QSA (Tvl).

HOWSE, Neville Reginald, 36
Captain, New South Wales Medical Staff Corps, Australian Forces.

(Wallace)

He was born at Stogursey in Somerset on Oct 26, 1863. The son of a surgeon, he qualified as a doctor in 1883. Dr Howse lived at Orange in Australia from 1889-95 then returned to London to practice. Howse qualified as a surgeon in 1897, then returned to Australia in 1899, where he was commissioned in the NSW Army Medical Corps. He was promoted captain and sent to serve in South Africa.

After the attack on May 28, 1900, by the Gordons on the Boer positions at Doornkop, south-east of Johannesburg, three doctors of the NSW Medical Corps assisted the wounded. Lieut Howse was one of them. They worked until 2.30 am in bell tents, using lamps and candles for lighting. He was then promoted captain.

On July 24 the NSW Mounted Rifles attacked Gen De Wet's rearguard near Vredefort, seven miles south of the Vaal River and south-west of Parys. De Wet retaliated and counter-attacked with Danie Theron's Scouts. A few hundred burghers and colonials faced each other on a small plain, often within

200 yards of each other, and fought for an hour. When two British guns were brought up the Boers withdrew. There were two killed on either side, although the colonials' casualties were 35 compared to the Boers 17.

Citation: During the action at Vredefort on the 24th July 1900, Capt Howse went out under a very heavy cross-fire, and picked up a wounded man and carried him to a place of shelter. (LG June 4, 1900).

Howse had galloped from the cover of a kraal to try to save a young wounded trumpeter. After his horse was shot Howse continued on foot across the bullet-swept ground. He bandaged the man and carried him back unaided through the cross-fire.

He was the first man to win a VC while serving in an Australian unit. Howse was invalided to Australia, but returned as a major to command the 1st Australian Commonwealth Bearer Company, part of the Australian Commonwealth Army Medical Corps.

In 1905 he married Evelyn Pilcher of Orange, NSW, and had two sons and three daughters. During World War I Col Howse served at Gallipoli with the ANZACs, landing on the first day. He was created a CB in Aug 1915 and in Dec 1915 promoted surgeon-general. He was attached to the HQ of the AIF in London, became a major-general and KCB in Jan 1917 and a KCMG in June 1919.

From 1927-8 Sir Neville was Minister for Defence and Health in Australia. In 1928 he was an Australian representative to the League of Nations Assembly. He died in London on Sep 19, 1930, aged 68 years. He is commemorated by a street being named after him in Canberra and in the VC Hall there, where his medals are on display. To date no other VC has been won by an Australian serving in a medical corps. An Australian postage stamp will feature his VC exploit in 2000.

OD&M: VC, KCMG, KCB, Knight of the Order of St John, QSA, KSA, 1914-15 Star, BWM, AVM (MID), Coronation Medal 1911.

HOUSE, William, 20
Private, 2nd Bn, The Royal Berkshire Regt

Born at Thatcham, near Newbury, Berkshire, on Oct
7, 1879, he joined the Royal Berkshire Regt (Princess
Charlotte of Wale's) in Nov 1896. He was to win fame
at Mosilikatse Nek (Silkaatsnek) in the Transvaal, 10
miles north-east of the present Hartebeespoort Dam in
the Magaliesberg, east of Pretoria.

(Creagh)

The name comes from Mzilikazi, the Matabele
chief, whom the Voortrekkers called Silkaats. On
July 11, 1900, Gen De la Rey scored a victory over the British at the pass. On
Aug 2 Gen Ian Hamilton re-took the pass, with the Argyl and Sutherland
Highlanders on the left and the Berkshires on the centre and right.

Citation: During the attack on Mosilikatse Nek, on the 2nd Aug. 1900, when a
sergeant, who had gone forward to reconnoitre, was wounded, Private House
rushed out from cover (though cautioned not to do so, as the fire from the
enemy was very hot), picked up the wounded sergeant, and endeavoured to
bring him into shelter, in doing which Private House was himself severely
wounded. He, however, warned his comrades not to come to his assistance,
the fire being so severe. The grant of the Medal for Distinguished Conduct in
the Field to Private House, which was notified in the London Gazette of the 27th
Sept. 1901, is hereby cancelled. (LG Oct 7, 1902).

The Boers abandoned their positions before midday and the Pass was secured.
House's VC was gazetted on his 23rd birthday. He subsequently served with
the 2nd Battalion in India and returned to England in Nov 1911. He was liable
to fits of depression while stationed at Dover's Shafts Barracks.

At Dover on Feb 28, 1912, while ostensibly cleaning his rifle it discharged
and shot him in the head, killing him. The *Dover Express* reported that he had
committed suicide "owing to his brain being unhinged either by the wound he
had received at the time he gained the VC, or from his subsequent service in
India." He is buried at St James's Cemetery, Dover. His medals are in the
Royal Berkshire Regimental Museum at Reading.

OD&M: VC, QSA, KSA (SA01, SA02), Coronation Medal 1911.

LAWRENCE, Brian Turner Tom, 26
Sergeant, 17th Lancers (Duke of Cambridge's Own)

Born at Bewdley, Worcestershire, on Nov 9, 1873, he
was to become an excellent horseman.   Tom
Lawrence joined the 17th Lancers and served in the
South African War.

(Creagh)

Citation: On the 7th Aug 1900, when on patrol duty
near Essenbosch Farm, Sergt Lawrence and a Private
(Hayman) were attacked by twelve or fourteen Boers.
Private Hayman's horse was shot, and the man was thrown, dislocating his
shoulder. Sergt Lawrence at once came to his assistance, extricated him from
under the horse, put him on his own horse, and sent him on to the picket. Sergt
Lawrence took the soldier's carbine, and with his own carbine as well, kept the
Boers off until Private Hayman was safely out of range. He then retired for
some two miles on foot, followed by the Boers, and keeping them off till
assistance arrived. (LG Jan 15, 1901).

Sergeant Lawrence was decorated by King Edward in London in Aug 1902.
He became a Sergeant and Riding Master in the 18th Hussars and was promoted
honorary lieutenant. Lawrence was a superb horseman and in 1912, at the
Stockholm Olympic Games, he was a member of the English riding team.
 Lawrence served in World War I and was dangerously wounded in 1914. He
was promoted captain in Dec 1915, major in 1917 and lieut-colonel (retired) in
1923. From 1923-6 he served on the General Staff, Iraq Levies, and in 1925-6
commanded a mobile column in Kurdistan.
 Lawrence married Nancy Leijel, born Mansfield, who died in 1944. From
1934-8 Lawrence was a Military Knight of Windsor. He served in World War
II at Whitehall until 1942. After visiting his younger brother, Capt Mark
Lawrence, in Kenya he decided to retire there. Lawrence died at Nakuru,
Kenya, on June 7, 1949, aged 75 years.

OD&M: VC, QSA (Cape, Jhbg, D Hill, Witt, SA01), 1914 Star (Mons clasp),
BWM, AVM (MID), Jubilee Medal 1935, Coronation Medal 1937, King
Feisal of Iraq War Medal, King Gustave V of Sweden Olympic Games Medal
1912. (He should be entitled to the Coronation Medal 1911, the 1939-45 Star
and 1939-45 War Medal).

HAMPTON, Harry, 29
Sergeant, 2nd Bn, The King's (Liverpool) Regt

He was born at Richmond, Surrey, on Dec 14, 1870.
Hampton joined the King's Liverpool Regiment at
Aldershot in March 1889 and served in the West
Indies and Nova Scotia from 1891-7. He then came
to South Africa and served through the Siege of
Ladysmith. He came under fire during the support of
the Wagon Hill defenders.

(Creagh)

After the siege he took part in the advance into the
Transvaal with the 1st Mounted Infantry Company of his Regiment. General
Buller left the Middelburg area and advanced north to reach Van Wyk's Vlei on
August 21. They were subjected to the fire of the Bethal Commando from
trenches on both sides of a ravine.

Citation: On the 21st Aug. 1900, at Van Wyk's Vlei, Sergt Hampton, who was
in command of a small party of Mounted Infantry, held an important position
for some time against heavy odds, and when compelled to retire saw all his
men into safety, and then, although he had himself been wounded in the head,
supported L-Corpl Walsh, who was unable to walk, until the latter was again
hit and apparently killed, Sergt Hampton himself being again wounded some
time after. (LG Oct 18, 1901).

The following day Gen W Kitchener attacked the Boers on the right flank and
forced them to withdraw. Sergeant Hampton was decorated by King Edward
VII at St James Palace. His was one of three VCs won by his regiment in three
days. Hampton became a colour-sergeant and sergeant instructor of musketry
before being discharged on pension. He had a son and a daughter.

Hampton was killed by falling against a passing steam train at Richmond,
London, on Feb 4, 1920, and was buried there in a pauper's grave, although he
was given a military funeral. Some allege that he committed suicide. In 1986
a local policeman located his grave and a headstone was erected. It is believed
that Hampton's distraught widow burnt his medals.

OD&M: VC, QSA (Defence of Ladysmith, Tvl), KSA (SA01, SA02),
Coronation Medal 1911.

KNIGHT, Henry James, 21
Corporal, 1ˢᵗ Bn, The King's (Liverpool) Regt

He was born at Yeovil, Somerset, on Nov 5, 1878, after his father had died. Knight joined the Liverpool Regiment and served in No 1 company, 4ᵗʰ Division, Mounted Infantry.

(Wilkins)

Citation: On the 21ˢᵗ Aug [1900] during the operations near Van Wyk's Vlei, Cpl Knight was posted in some rocks with four men, covering the right rear of a detachment of the same company, who, under Capt Ewart, were holding the right of the line. The enemy, about fifty strong, attacked Capt Ewart's right and almost surrounded, at short range, Cpl Knight's small party. That non-commissioned officer held his ground, directing his party to retire one by one to better cover, while he maintained his position for nearly an hour, covering the withdrawal of Capt Ewart's force, and losing two of his four men. He then retired, bringing with him two wounded men. One of these he left in a place of safety, the other he carried for nearly two miles. The party were hotly engaged during the whole time. (LG Jan 4, 1901).

Knight was promoted sergeant and decorated by Lord Kitchener at Pretoria on June 8, 1902. He joined the Manchester Regiment in Feb 1915 as a temporary lieutenant and by March was a captain. He testified in a scandal involving illicit payments made by his regiment, then in Oct 1915 relinquished his commission.

The following month he joined the London Scottish as a private. He was promoted corporal and sent to France, where he was wounded at Gommecourt in July 1916. He died at Winterbome, Anderson, near Blandford, Dorset, on Nov 24, 1955, aged 77 years, and was cremated at Bournemouth Cemetery.

OD&M: VC, QSA (Def of Ladysmith, Laing's Nek, Belfast, OFS), KSA (SA01, SA02), 1914-15 Star, BWM, AVM, Coronation Medals 1911, 1937 and 1953, LSGC (George V). The 1914-15 Star and 1911 Coronation Medal are not with his group.

HEATON, William Edward, 25
Private, 1ˢᵗ Bn, The King's (Liverpool) Regt

(Wilkins)

He was born in 1875 at Ormskirk, Lancashire. At age 25 he found himself serving as a private in the 8ᵗʰ (The King's Liverpool) Regiment. The Battle of Bergendal would take place on August 27. As one of the preliminaries Gen Buller advanced to Geluk farm on the 23ʳᵈ and found the ridge to the north occupied by the Heidelberg Commando. His artillery dueled with the Long Tom on the ridge and grievously wounded its artillery commander, Von Dalwig.

Two companies of the Liverpools at the nearby Leeukloof Farm, eight miles south of Belfast, became cut off and were subjected to heavy rifle fire. They kept the Boers at bay until their ammunition began to fail and the Boers enveloped their flanks.

Citation: On the 23ʳᵈ August 1900, the company to which Private Heaton belonged, advancing in front of the general line held by the troops, became surrounded by the enemy and was suffering severely. At the request of the officer commanding, Private Heaton volunteered to take a message back to explain the position of the company. He was successful, though at the imminent risk of his own life. Had it not been for Private Heaton's courage, there can be little doubt that the remainder of the company, which suffered very severely, would have had to surrender. (LG Jan 18, 1901).

At dusk the two companies began retiring, covered by a few men. They lost ten killed, 48 wounded and 30 missing. Meanwhile Buller had held his position on a ridge north of the farm.

Heaton was decorated at Pietermaitzburg by the Duke of Cornwall and York on Aug 14. 1901. He was later promoted sergeant. He died at Southport, Lancashire, on June 5, 1941, aged 66 years. His wife, Elizabeth, died in Jan 1953 and is buried alongside him. His medals belong to the King's Regiment and are deposited at the Liverpool Museum.

OD&M: VC, QSA (Three clasps), KSA (SA01, SA02), 1914-15 Star, BWM, AVM, Coronation Medal 1937.

DURRANT, Alfred Edward, 35
Private, 2nd Bn The Rifle Brigade

He was born at St James's, Westminster, London, on
Nov 4, 1864. Durrant enlisted in the Rifle Brigade
(Prince Consort's Own) and served in the operations
leading to the taking of Pretoria and pursuit of the
Boers into the Eastern Transvaal.

The Battle of Bergendal, near Belfast, was to be the
last set-piece battle and decisive engagement before
the Boers began their guerrilla campaign. After

(Creagh)

bombarding the Boers central positions, where the Zarps (ZAR Police) held on
doggedly, the Inniskillings and Rifle Brigade made a frontal assault.

Citation: At Bergendal on the 27th Aug 1900, Acting-Corpl Wellar, having
been wounded and being somewhat dazed, got up from his prone position in
the firing line, exposing himself still more to the enemy's fire, and commenced
to run towards them. Private Durrant rose, and, pulling him down,
endeavoured to keep him quiet, but finding this impossible, he took him up and
carried him back for 200 yards under a heavy fire to shelter, returning
immediately to his place in the line. (LG Oct 18, 1901).

The successful taking of this position was the deciding factor in the battle. The
Boers then withdrew from their positions. Durrant was promoted lance-
corporal. It took almost a year and two months before his VC award was
promulgated. He died at Tottenham, London, on March 29, 1933, aged 68.

OD&M: VC, ISM, QSA (Three clasps), KSA (SA01, SA02), Coronation
Medal 1911, LSGC (Edward VII).

WYLLY, Guy George Egerton, 20
Lieutenant, Tasmanian Imperial Bushmen

Born on Feb 17, 1880, at Hobart, Tasmania, he was
the son of Major Edward Wylly, formerly of the 109th
Regt and Madras Staff Corps.   His maternal
grandfather served as Sergeant-at-Arms to the House
of Assembly in Hobart.   In April 1900 Wylly became
a lieutenant in the Tasmanian Bushmen.

(Creagh)

On September 1, 1900, Major E Brooke led a party
of Army Service Corps men foraging near Warm Bad
(Warm Bath), near Belfast.   They were escorted by a troop of Tasmanian
Imperial Bushmen commanded by Lieut Wylly.   He was leading a party of
eight scouts when they were ambushed at point-blank range.   Major Brooke
and Lieut Wylly were among the six men wounded, while three of their horses
were killed.

Citation: On the 1st Sept 1900, near Warm Bad, Lieut Wylly was with the
advanced scouts of a foraging party.   They were passing through a narrow
gorge, very rocky and thickly wooded, when the enemy in force suddenly
opened fire at short range from hidden cover, wounding six out of the party of
eight, including Lieut Wylly.   That officer, seeing that one of his men was
badly wounded in the leg, and that his horse was shot, went back to the man's
assistance, made him take his (Lieut Wylly's) horse, and opened fire from
behind a rock to cover the retreat of the others, at the imminent risk of being cut
off himself.   Colonel T E Hickman, DSO, considers that the gallant conduct of
Lieut Wylly saved Corpl Brown from being killed or captured, and that his
subsequent action in firing to cover the retreat was instrumental in saving
others of his men from death or capture. (LG Nov 23, 1900).

When Lieut Wylly rescued Cpl E S Brown the man was wearing a leather
money belt around his ankle.   When a mauser bullet struck his leg it cut a piece
out of the sovereign in the belt, leaving the coin sticking in his wound.

While Wylly covered the retreat of the party with rifle fire, he was joined by
Trooper F Groom, who was later awarded the DCM.   Corporal E Brown's
brother, Trooper G Brown, later died of his wounds.   Wylly was decorated by
King Edward VII at St James Palace, London, on July 25, 1901.

Wylly transferred to the Berkshires, then the Lancashire Regt, with whom he
served in India from Dec 1901.   He was gazetted to the 46th Punjabis in Oct
1902, then two years later served with the Queen's Own Corps of Guides.

From 1904-9 he was ADC to Lord Kitchener in India. From 1915-16 Wylly

69

was ADC to the commander of the Northern Army, India, and was seriously wounded in the face at Authoille in Aug 1915. In June 1916 Major Wylly was GSO2 to the 4th Division, BEF, and from July he became GSO2 to the Anzac Corps. For his services in France Wylly was created a companion of the DSO in Jan 1918.

He served on the North-West Frontier of India from 1919-30, commanding the DCO Lancers from 1926-9. From 1926-33 Wylly was ADC to the king, while serving as Assistant Adjutant and QMG of the Peshawar District. He died at Camberley, Surrey, on Jan 9, 1962. There is a memorial to him at St John's Crematorium, Woking, Surrey.

OD&M: VC, CB, DSO, QSA, Delhi Durbar Medal (1911), 1914-15 Star, BWM, AVM, IGS (Bar Waziristan 1919-21), Coronation Medals 1911, 1937 and 1953.

BISDEE, John Hutton, 30
Trooper, 1st Tasmanian Imperial Bushmen

He was born at Hutton Park, Tasmania, on Sep 28, 1869. While both his parents had been born in Tasmania, his grandparents had come from Hutton, Somersetshire. He enlisted in a Tasmanian unit for service in South Africa.

Trooper Bisdee was with Lieut Wylly's advance party of scouts near Warm Bad when they were ambushed. The Army Service Corps commander, Major Eardley Brooke, was hit and his horse bolted.

(Wilkins)

Citation: On the 1st Sept 1900, Trooper Bisdee was one of an advanced scouting party passing through a rocky defile near Warm Bad, Transvaal. The enemy, who were in ambuscade, opened a sudden fire at close range, and six out of the party of eight were hit, including two officers. The horse of one of the wounded officers broke away and bolted. Finding that the officer was too badly wounded to go on, Trooper Bisdee dismounted, placed him on his horse, mounted behind him, and conveyed him out of range. This act was performed under a very hot fire, and in a very exposed place. (LG Nov 13, 1900).

He was wounded in the ambush and invalided home. Bisdee was the first Australian to receive the VC while serving in an Australian unit under British command. His award was gazetted 10 days before Lieut Wylly's. In March 1901 Bisdee was commissioned in the 2nd Tasmanian Imperial Bushmen and returned to serve for the duration of the war.

He thereafter returned to farming in Tasmania. In April 1904 Bisdee married Georgina Hale. Two years later he joined the 12th Australian Light Horse. By 1912 he commanded the 26th Light Horse Regt in Tasmania.

Major Bisdee served with the 12th Australian Light Horse, Australian Composite Regt, in Dec 1915 in the Egyptian Senussi Campaign. He was wounded in the leg at Mersa Matruh, which precluded him from further active service. He was promoted lieut-colonel in Feb 1918 and awarded the OBE (Military Division) in June 1919.

Fond of sport, especially football, and hunting he died at Melton Mowbray, Tasmania, on Jan 14, 1930, aged 60. He is remembered by the Bisdee Memorial Cadet Efficiency Prize at St Virgil's College, Hobart, and at VC Corner, Australian War Memorial, Canberra.

OD&M: VC, OBE (Military Division), QSA (Two clasps), KSA (SA01, SA02), 1914-15 Star, BWM, AVM, Coronation Medal 1911.

(Wallace)

Trooper Bisdee welcomed home.

BROWN (Later **Brown-Synge-Hutchinson**),
Edward Douglas, 39
Major, 14th Hussars

He was born in Dagshai, India, on March 6, 1861, son
of Major David Brown (7th Queen's Own Hussars) and
Frances, sister of Sir Edward Synge-Hutchinson, 4th
Baronet. He was commissioned in the 18th Hussars in
Nov 1883 and was a captain within five years. He
grew an enormous moustache to conceal a sword cut.

(Wilkins)

After exchanging into the 14th Hussars in March 1889 he commanded the
Aldershot School of Instruction for Yeomanry. He became a major in Jan
1899. He was mentioned in despatches for the retirement at Thaba Nchu, and
for leading the most advanced position at the Battle of Diamond Hill under
heavy fire.

The engagement for which he earned the VC appears to have taken place on
the same farm, Geluk, that Private Heaton had won the award two months
before.

Citation: On the 13th Oct 1900, at Geluk, when the enemy were within 400
yards, and bringing a heavy fire to bear, Major Brown, seeing that Sergt
Hersey's horse was shot, stopped behind the last squadron, as it was retiring,
and helped Sergt Hersey to mount behind him, carrying him for about three
quarters of a mile to a place of safety. He did this under a heavy fire. Major
Brown afterwards enabled Lieut Browne, 14th Hussars, to mount, by holding
his horse, which was very restive under the heavy fire. Lieut Browne could not
otherwise have mounted. Subsequently Major Brown carried L-Corpl
Trumpeter Leigh out of action. (LG Jan 15, 1901).

The citation doesn't mention that Major Brown held the horses of three other
men who were having difficulty. He was the last officer of the British regular
army to win the VC during the life of Queen Victoria, and one of the oldest at
37 years 8 months. He regarded it as "about the limit of antiquity for this
decoration."

Brown was decorated by the Duke of Cornwall and York (later George V) at
Pietermaritzburg on Aug 14, 1901. He was promoted lieut-colonel and
commanded the 14th Hussars. Brown changed his name to Browne-Synge-
Hutchinson. By 1911 he was a CB, a colonel, a Knight of Grace of the Order of
St John of Jerusalem and a Freeman of the city of London. In 1917 he was
promoted Knight of Justice of the Order of St John of Jerusalem. Brown-
Synge-Hutchinson was an avid medal collector. He died in London on Feb 3,
1940, aged 78 years.

OD&M: VC, CB, QSA (Cape, Tug Hts, OFS, Rel of Ladysmith, Jhbg, D Hill, Belfast), KSA (SA01, SA02), Coronation Medal 1937, Knight of the Order of St John of Jerusalem.

(After Pretoria)

Major Brown holding Lieutenant Browne's Horse under fire.

DOXAT, Alexis Charles, 33
Lieutenant, 3rd Bn, Imperial Yeomanry

He was born at Surbiton, Surrey, on April 9, 1867.
Doxat served as a captain in the Dalston Militia and
passed the Auxiliary School of Instruction and the
Musketry School. Although a member of the stock
exchange, he resigned in order to serve in South
Africa.

(The Register)

From May 1900 Lieut Doxat took part in Lord
Methuen's advance from Boshof. In September he
joined General Douglas's column in the western Transvaal as personal ADC,
though he acted as reconnaissance officer.

Citation: On the 20th October 1900, near Zeerust, Lieut Doxat proceeded with
a party of mounted infantry to reconnoitre a position held by 100 Boers on a
ridge of kopjes. When within 300 yards of the position the enemy opened a
heavy fire on Lieut Doxat's party, which then retired, leaving one of their
number who had lost his horse. Lieut Doxat, seeing the dangerous position in
which the man was placed, galloped back under a very heavy fire, and brought
him on his horse to a place of safety. (LG Jan 15, 1901).

He was the first Yeoman and the first member of the Stock Exchange to win the
VC. Doxat was decorated with the VC by King Edward VII at Marlborough
House on Dec 17, 1901. He married Mrs Hugh Mair and served in World War
I. Honorary Major Doxat was invalided out of the army in 1918. He died at
Cambridge on Nov 29, 1942, aged 75. His medals were sold by Sothebys in
1971 for £1,900.

OD&M: VC, QSA (Cape, OFS, Tvl, SA01), 1914-15 Star, BWM, AVM,
Coronation Medal 1937.

COCKBURN, Hampden Zane Churchill, 32
Lieutenant, Royal Canadian Dragoons

He was born at Toronto, Canada, on Nov 19, 1867, the
son of a former MP and bank director. Educated at
Toronto and Rugby School in England, he was
commissioned in the Governor General's Bodyguards
in 1891. In Sep 1897 Cockburn earned the Canadian
Humane Society's Medal for saving two brothers who
were drowning in Lake Rousseau, Canada.

(Wilkins)

Three years later his valour was tested in South
Africa. At Liliefontein, Komati River, near Belfast, General Smith-Dorrien
had forced the Boers out of a strong position, which they attempted to recover
the next day, after they had been reinforced. They were forestalled by the guns
of the 84th Battery. On the return march the Canadian Dragoons acted as
rearguard when attacked by 200 Boers. Despite being outnumbered, they
behaved well and earned three VCs.

Citation: Date of Act of Bravery: 7 Nov 1900. Lieut Cockburn with a
handful of men, at a most critical moment, held off the Boers to allow the guns
to get away. To do so he had to sacrifice himself and his party, all of whom
were killed, wounded or taken prisoner, he himself being slightly wounded.
(LG April 23, 1901).

The brief citation does little credit to Lieut Cockburn, Lieut Turner and Sgt
Holland who won VCs in the gallant defence of the guns at Komati River.
Cockburn commanded a troop of the Dragoons in 45 engagements and
marches totaling 1,700 miles.

He was decorated with the VC by HRH the Duke of Cornwall and York at
Toronto on Oct 11, 1901. On the same occasion a sword of honour was
presented to him by the city. Major Cockburn belonged to the Canadian
Reserve of Officers. He was killed by his horse at his ranch at Maple Creek on
July 13, 1913, and is buried in St James's Cemetery, Toronto.

OD&M: VC, QSA (Cape, Johannesburg, Diamond Hill, OFS), Coronation
Medal 1911, Canadian Royal Humane Society Medal.

TURNER, Richard Ernest William, 29
Lieutenant, 13th Royal Canadian Dragoons

The son of a MLC he was born at Quebec on July 25,
1871. He was commissioned in the Royal Canadian
Dragoons and present with them in the rearguard
action at Liliefontein, Komati River.

One of his men, Trooper Hilder, recalled, "The guns
were in grave danger of being captured. Lieutenant
Turner galloped up and shouted, 'Dismount and hold
back the enemy!' I remember distinctly him saying,

(Wilkins)

'Never let it be said the Canadians had let their guns be taken' ... Again Lieut
Turner galloped up, now seriously wounded in the neck and his arm shattered
... But the important thing was, the guns of D Battery had not been captured;
they had been saved by the stubborn resistance of the RCD."

Turner's diary recorded, "Then things began to happen. About 200 mounted
Boers charged down on our rearguard shooting wildly from horseback in an
effort to capture our two guns. In the meantime I had picked up a bullet in my
left arm but used this as an example to the men to rally. As we fell back, I
dismounted the handful with me, about a dozen men and then just got another
bullet through my neck [my] horse was twice wounded."

Citation: Date of act of bravery 7 Nov 1900. Later in the day when the Boers
again threatened seriously to capture the guns, Lieut Turner, although twice
previously wounded, dismounted and deployed his men at close quarters, and
drove off the Boers, thus saving the guns. (LG April 23, 1901).

The rearguard was abandoned by British infantry. When Lieut Turner heard of
this he rallied 12 Canadians and appealed to their patriotism. Using his wound
as an example he shouted, "Never let it be said that the Canadians let their guns
be captured." They then ambushed 100 men of the Carolina Commando,
killing their commander.

Turner received another wound, in his neck, and was captured with his
surviving men but later released with them. The Boers were impressed by the
Canadians and treated them so humanely that they were specially thanked by
General Smith-Dorrien afterwards.

Turner was later mentioned in despatches three times and promoted lieut-
colonel. In 1900 he married Harriet Gooday of London and had a son and a
daughter. On April 19, 1901, Turner was created a Companion of the DSO.
During World War I he commanded the 3rd Canadian Infantry Brigade in
France until Aug 1915, then as a major-general commanded the 2nd Canadian
Division for over a year.

Turner was recalled to England in 1917 to command the Canadian Forces in Great Britain. By June 1917 he was a lieut-general and by May 1918 Chief of the General Staff Overseas Military Forces of Canada. For his services he was mentioned in despatches and created a CB and a KCMG.

Lieut-Gen Sir Richard Turner attended the 1956 VC Reunion in London. Among his medals was the Colonial Auxiliary Forces Officers Decoration (VD). He died at Quebec on June 29, 1961, and is buried in the Mt Hermon Cemetery there. His medals were bequeathed to the Royal Canadian Dragoons Museum in New Brunswick.

OD&M: VC, KCB, KCMG, CB, DSO, VD, QSA (Cape, OFS, Jhbg, D Hill, Belfast), 1914-15 Star, BWM, AVM, Coronation Medals 1911, 1937 and 1953, Canadian Forces Decoration, Legion d'Honneur, Croix de Guerre avec palme (France), Order of the White Eagle with Swords (Russia).

HOLLAND, Edward James Gibson, 22
Sergeant, Royal Canadian Dragoons

He was born at Ottawa, Canada, on Feb 2, 1878. Sergeant Holland was with the Royal Canadian Dragoons at Komati River when the guns were threatened.

(Wilkins)

Citation: Date of Act of Bravery 7 Nov 1900. Sergeant Holland did splendid work with his colt-gun, and kept the Boers off the two 12-pounders by its fire at close range. When he saw the enemy were too near for him to escape with the carriage, as the horse was blown, he calmly lifted the gun off and galloped away with it under his arm. (LG April 23, 1901).

Holland had waited until his pursuers were within 200 yards of his Colt, then unscrewed the barrel from its carriage, put it under his arm and galloped off. His exploit occurred shortly before Lieut Turner set up his ambush.

Holland returned to Canada and from 1909 prospected for gold, taking part in the Gillies Limit Rush three years later. He later became a major with the 13th Canadian Dragoons, and took a battery of mounted machine-guns to France in Sep 1915, returning to Canada in Oct 1916 as a lieut-colonel, where he served in the Reserves.

As a businessman he sold typewriters and cash registers in the Pacific and also served as a postman in Cobalt, Ontario. Holland married Dora Knapp and had two sons and a daughter. A son, William, was killed in a plane crash in British Columbia. Holland died at Cobalt on June 18, 1948, and his ashes were scattered on Island 17, Lake Temagami, Ontario.

OD&M: VC, QSA, 1914-15 Star, BWM, AVM, Coronation Medals 1911 and 1937.

KENNEDY, Charles Thomas, 27
Private, 2nd Bn, The Highland Light Infantry

He was born at Westport, Edinburgh, on Jan 6, 1873, one of 13 children of whom only four survived to adulthood. Kennedy went into the furniture trade, but during the 1891 depression joined the Highland Light Infantry in Glasgow for service in India.

He played half-back for the HLI soccer team, which won the Durand Cup in 1895. Kennedy served in the

(Wilkins)

Malakand Field Force before returning to Scotland in 1898. He rejoined for service in South Africa and was present at the fighting near Dewetsdorp, 25 miles south-east of Thaba Nchu, where he was to display extreme valour.

Citation: At Dewetsdorp on the 22nd Nov 1900, Private Kennedy carried a comrade, who was dangerously wounded and bleeding to death, from Gibraltar Hill to the hospital, a distance of three-quarters of a mile, under a very hot fire. On the following day, volunteers having been called for to take a message to the Commandant across a space over which it was almost certain death to venture, Private Kennedy at once stepped forward. He did not, however, succeed in delivering the message, as he was severely wounded before he had gone twenty yards. (LG Oct 18, 1901).

Kennedy was hospitalised in Bloemfontein, then sent to Aldershot in April 1901. He was decorated by King Edward VII on Dec 17, 1901, at St James Palace. He was then discharged from the army on account of poor health and returned to live in Edinburgh.

At Edinburgh on April 24, 1907, he was again called on to show his bravery. A horse bolted with a contractor's cart in Leith Walk, and in attempting to stop it he was knocked down and the wheels passed over him. Kennedy died on the way to the Royal Infirmary, and is buried in the North Merchiston Cemetery, Edinburgh.

OD&M: VC, IGS 1895 (Malakand 1897), QSA (Modder River, Paardeberg, Wittebergen).

FARMER, Donald Dickson, 23
Sergeant, 1ˢᵗ Bn, Cameron Highlanders

He was born on May 28, 1877, at Kelso, Roxburghshire, Scotland. He joined the Queen's Own Cameron Hldrs in March 1892 and served with the 1ˢᵗ Battalion in the Sudan Campaign, being present at the Battles of Atbara and Khartoum and the affair at Fashoda. In South Africa he served with the Mounted Infantry Company.

(Rustenburg)

Lord Kitchener sent Gen Clements to clear the Magaliesberg, between Pretoria and Rustenburg, of Boers. He camped on the farm Nooitgedacht, overlooked by the mountains and a Nek, which would be difficult to defend. At 3.45 am on December 13 they were attacked by combined commandos under Generals De la Rey, Beyers and Smuts.

While Beyers attacked over the mountain from the north-west, Smuts came from the north-east and De la Rey from the south-west. The latter initially attacked the Mounted Infantry camp, in which Sgt Farmer slept. The commander, Brigadier-General Norton Legge DSO, ran from his tent and was killed. The Boers also suffered casualties and withdrew in order to coordinate the assault better.

Beyers attacked the British on the mountain and by 7 am had overrun their positions. The main attack on the Nooitgedacht camp then commenced.

Citation: During the attack on General Clements camp at Nooitgedacht, on the 13ᵗʰ Dec 1900, Lieut Sandilands, Cameron Highlanders, with fifteen men, went to the assistance of a picquet [picket] which was heavily engaged, most of the men having been killed or wounded. The enemy, who were hidden by trees, opened fire on the party at a range of about twenty yards, killing two and wounding five, including Lieut Sandilands. Sergt Farmer at once went to the officer, who was perfectly helpless, and carried him away under a very heavy and close fire to a place of comparative safety, after which he returned to the firing line, and was eventually taken prisoner. (LG April 12, 1901).

According to Lionel Wulfsohn in 'Rustenburg at War': "Sergeant Donald Farmer of the 1ˢᵗ Battalion Cameron Highlanders was awarded the VC for his gallantry in assisting a wounded officer to a field ambulance, and then returning to the front line distributing bandoliers of cartridges, which he had taken from the dead and wounded, to those who could still handle a rifle..."

Lieutenant Sandilands had been shot through the liver and both shoulders. Sergeant Farmer was the first Cameron Highlander to win the VC. He was presented with his VC by the Duke of York on Aug 14, 1901, at Pietermaritzburg. In 1903 he married Helen Bonnar and they had a son and three daughters.

Donald Farmer became a colour-sergeant in Feb 1905 and was later commissioned, eventually retiring as a lieut-colonel. He achieved his wish of attending the VC and GC Reunion in June 1956, before his sight failed him completely. He died at Liverpool, Lancashire, on Dec 23, 1965, aged 88, and was cremated.

OD&M: VC, MSM, Queen's Sudan Medal, Khedive's Medal (Two clasps), QSA (Four clasps), KSA (SA01, SA02), 1914-15 Star, BWM, AVM, Coronation Medals 1937 and 1953, LSGC.

1901

BARRY, John, 27
Private, 1ˢᵗ Bn, The Royal Irish Regiment

John Barry was born at Kilkenny, Ireland, on Feb 1, 1873. He joined the Royal Irish Regt in Dec 1890 and served on the North-West Frontier of India and in the Punjab. He transferred to South Africa and served extensively. It was two miles north-west of Belfast, Transvaal, that he won the supreme award.

(Wilkins)

Citation: During the night attack on the 7ᵗʰ-8ᵗʰ Jan 1901, on Monument Hill, Private Barry, although surrounded and threatened by the Boers at the time, smashed the breach of the maxim gun, thus rendering it useless to its captors, and it was in doing this splendid act for his country that he met his death. (LG Aug 8, 1902).

According to the Times History (Vol V p 123), "Muller's [Gen C H Muller] men effected a complete surprise, overpowered the sentries at Monument Hill and stumbling through the wire fencing, threw themselves upon the fort. Some were caught in the wire, many were shot down, but the greater number reached the walls and began to climb over them, firing down upon the defenders.

"Heavily outnumbered, [Capt} Fosbery and his men fought desperately to the bitter end, some men laying about them with the butt end of their rifles and others using their fists or wrestling with the enemy. In this brief but bloody struggle Fosbery fell dead and 39 of his [83] men were killed or wounded.

"One of the maxim detachment, Private J Barry, when all his comrades were down, seized a pick and began to smash up the breech of the gun. Called on to stop, he persisted until he had rendered the gun useless, when the Boers, robbed of their spoil, shot him dead..."

John Barry is buried in the Belfast old municipal cemetery, Mpumalanga. His medals were sold for £70 by his mother, Mrs Catherine Barry, in 1907. In 1986 they were resold by Donald Hall.

OD&M: VC, IGS 1895 (Sawana 1897, Punjab 1897-8), QSA (Cape, Wittebergen, Belfast).

HARDHAM, William James, 24
Farrier Sgt-Major, 4th New Zealand Contingent

He was born at Wellington, New Zealand, on July 31, 1876, although his parents had come from Surrey, England. Hardham joined the Cadets in 1891 and served in the Petone Naval Artillery Volunteers from 1894. From 1897 he represented Wellington Province at rugby.

(Creagh)

Hardham then came to South Africa with the New Zealand Contingent. His service was almost totally in the Transvaal, except for the following engagement at Noupoort, south of Colesberg:

Citation: On the 28th Jan 1901, near Naauwpoort, this non-commissioned officer was with a section which was extended and hotly engaged with a party of about twenty Boers. Just before the force commenced to retire Trooper McCrae was wounded and his horse killed. Farrier-Major Hardham at once went under a heavy fire to his assistance, dismounted, and placed him on his own horse, and ran alongside until he had guided him to a place of safety. (LG Oct 4, 1901).

Hardham was decorated by the Prince of Wales in London on July 1, 1902, together with Bell, English and Clements. He was the first New Zealand-born man to win the VC. Abbott & Tamplin refer to him in error as Hardman. They record that he was issued with an unnamed VC in 1902, which he subsequently had incorrectly engraved with his name behind the cross and the date behind the clasp.

He continued playing rugby for Wellington, often as captain, until 1910. In 1904 he played against England. Captain Hardham served with the New Zealand Mounted Rifles at Gallipoli and was wounded in May 1915, then invalided to New Zealand.

He later became Military Commandant of the Queen Mary Hospital for sick and wounded returned soldiers in New Zealand. In March 1916 Hardham married Constance Parsonstown. He returned to Europe with reinforcements in Feb 1918. Major Hardham joined the Reserve of Officers in Oct 1919. He died at Wellington on April 13, 1928, aged 51, and is buried in the Soldiers' Cemetery, Karori, Wellington. His name is on a commemorative plaque outside the [Army] HQ, Dunedin, New Zealand.

OD&M: VC, QSA (Five clasps), 1914-15 Star, BWM, AVM, Coronation Medals 1902 and 1911.

TRAYNOR, William Bernard, 30
Sergeant, 2nd Bn, The West Yorkshire Regiment

He was born at Hull, Yorkshire, on Dec 31, 1870, and educated in a Roman Catholic school. Traynor joined the 2nd Bn, West Yorkshire Regt, in Nov 1888 and served in India. He married Jane Martin in June 1897 and they had four sons and two daughters. One of his daughters died shortly after the Battle of Colenso.

(Wilkins)

In South Africa Traynor fought in the major Natal battles (Colenso, Spion Kop, Vaalkrantz and Pieters Hill), then northern Natal, Orange River Colony and Transvaal. He proved his mettle when Major-General Smith-Dorrien was attacked at Bothwell Camp, Lake Chrissie, 20 miles north-east of Ermelo.

The Boers, led by Gen Louis Botha, attacked in the dark before dawn and got through two picquets, having followed up 200 stampeding cavalry horses. There was murderous fire from both sides.

Citation: During the night attack on Bothwell Camp, on the 6th February, 1901, Sergt Traynor jumped out of a trench and ran out under an extremely heavy fire to the assistance of a wounded man. While running out he was severely wounded, and being unable to carry the man by himself, he called for assistance. L-Corpl Lintott at once came to him, and between them they carried the wounded soldier into shelter. After this, although severely wounded, Sergt Traynor remained in command of his section, and was most cheerful in encouraging his men till the attack failed. (LG Sept 17, 1901).

Corporal Lintott was awarded the DCM for assisting Sergeant Traynor. The War Office sent a telegram to Mrs Traynor announcing with regret that he had been killed in action. Traynor's wounds were so serious that he was invalided to England and discharged as medically unfit in Sep 1901. As he was unable to travel to London to receive his decoration from the king, Traynor was presented with his VC at York by Col Edward Stevenson Browne VC (of Zulu War fame).

The following year he was employed as Barrack Warden at Dover, Kent, and during the First World War was mentioned for valuable services. He died at Dover on Oct 20, 1956, aged 83 years, and is buried in the Charlton Cemetery. He had twin sons, both of whom served as majors in the Royal Engineers.

OD&M: VC, India Medal, QSA (Tugela Heights, Relief of Ladysmith, Laings Nek, Transvaal, OFS), KSA (SA01).

CLEMENTS, John James, 28
Corporal, Rimington's Guides, South African Forces

Born at Middelburg, Cape, on June 19, 1872, he was a
good boxer and always ready for a fight! He was
serving under Major Damant in 'Rimington's Tigers'
when his patrol ran into six Boers on a kopje about
four miles (8 km) south of Strijdenburg, Cape (55 km
south-west of Hopetown and the Orange River). His
officer, Lieut Harvey, was mortally wounded.

(Uys)

Citation: On the 24th Feb 1900 [sic 1901], near Strijdenburg, when
dangerously wounded through the lungs, and called upon to surrender, Corpl
Clements threw himself into the midst of a party of five of five Boers, shooting
three of them with his revolver, and thereby causing the whole party to
surrender to himself and two unwounded men of Rimington's Guides. (LG
June 4, 1901).

Clements had himself been dangerously wounded before he attacked the
Boers. Two Boers were killed and four captured. He thereafter served as a
sergeant in Damant's Horse. He was presented with the VC by the Prince of
Wales in London in July 1902, at the same time as Lieut Bell.
    He married Florence Palmer and had five children. Clements served in
Botha's Scouts during the German South West Africa Campaign. His wife
died in 1917 and he remarried and had a further three children.
    Clements farmed near Newcastle, Natal, where he died on June 18, 1937, the
day before his 65th birthday. The local MOTHs erected a tombstone over his
grave. His medals were sold in October 1999 for £65,000.

OD&M: VC, QSA (Belmont, Modder River, Relief of Kimberley,
Paardeberg, Driefontein, Johannesburg, Diamond Hill, Wittebergen), KSA
(SA01, SA02), Coronation Medals 1902 and 1911.

DUGDALE, Frederic Brooks, 23
Lieutenant, 5th Lancers (Royal Irish)

A son of Col James Dugdale VD, he was born at Burnley, Lancashire, on Oct 21, 1877. After an education at Marlborough and Oxford he was commissioned in the 5th Lancers. On arrival in South Africa his regiment took part in the Relief of Ladysmith.

(The Register)

Dugdale continued serving with the relieving force under General Buller and was promoted lieutenant in May 1900. He then served under General French in the Cape. His VC engagement took place at Derby, east of Krugersdorp, Transvaal.

Citation: On 3 March 1901, Lieut Dugdale, who was in command of a small outpost near Derby, having been ordered to retire, his patrol came under a heavy fire at a range of about 250 yards, and a sergeant, two men, and a horse were hit. Lieut Dugdale dismounted and placed one of the wounded men on his own horse; he then caught another horse, galloped up to a wounded man and took him up behind him, and brought both men safely out of action. (LG Sep 17, 1901).

Dugdale then caught enteric fever. On regaining his health he served with Gen French in the Cape. He returned to England in July 1902 and in October was decorated with the VC by King Edward VII at Buckingham Palace. On Nov 13, 1902, while hunting with the North Cotswold, his horse fell at a fence and crushed him so severely that he died within two hours, without regaining consciousness. He is buried at Longborough, Gloucestershire.

His brother, Arthur (1869-1941) was awarded the CMG in 1915 and commanded the Queen's Own Oxfordshire Hussars. Another brother, James, born in 1874, earned the DSO in 1902 and the MVO in 1917 while a major in the 18th Hussars.

OD&M: VC, QSA (Tugela Heights, Relief of Ladysmith, Laings Nek, OFS, Belfast, Cape).

BELL, Frederick William, 26
Lieutenant, West Australian Mounted Infantry

He was born at Perth, West Australia, on April 3, 1875. Bell was commissioned in the West Australian Mounted Infantry and earned his VC at the Brakpan Farm in the Eastern Transvaal.

Citation: At Brakpan on the 16th May 1901, when retiring through a heavy fire after holding the right flank, Lieut Bell noticed a man dismounted, and returned and took him up behind him. The horse, not being equal to the weight, fell with them. Lieut Bell then remained behind, and covered the man's retirement till he was out of danger. (LG Oct 4, 1901).

(Wilkins)

He was decorated by the Prince of Wales (King George V) in London on July 11, 1902. In 1915 he became a temporary captain in command of a rest camp, then served as commandant, Embarkation Camps, at Plymouth.

Lieut-Colonel Bell was an administrative officer in British Somaliland, Northern Nigeria and Kenya and served in the Reserve of Officers during World War II. His first wife died in 1944 and he then married a widow, Brenda Cracklow. He had no children. During an investigation he criticised the colonial office's attitude toward the Swahili, so was recalled and pensioned off.

Bell died at Westbury-on-Trym on April 28, 1954, aged 79 years, and is buried in Canford Cemetery, near Bristol. His name is also commemorated in the VC Corner, Australian War Memorial, Canberra. His medals are on display at the West Australian Museum at Perth.

OD&M: VC, QSA (Cape, Jhbg, D Hill, Witt), KSA (SA01, SA02), Africa General Service Medal (Somaliland 1908-10), 1914-15 Star, BWM, AVM (MID), Coronation Medals 1902, 1937 and 1953.

COULSON, Gustavus Hamilton Blenkinsopp, 22, DSO
Lieutenant, 1ˢᵗ Bn, The King's Own Scottish Borderers

A grandson of Col Blenkinsopp Coulson of Blenkinsopp Castle, Northumberland, he was born at Wimbledon, Surrey, on April 1, 1879. He joined the 4ᵗʰ Bn Yorkshire Regt but transferred to the KOSB in July 1899. Coulson went on active service to South Africa in Jan 1900 and was promoted lieutenant in July.

(The Register)

According to Dooner, "He was present at the Battle of Paardeberg, where he had his horse shot under him in the charge in which Col Hannay fell. He then remained out, shooting Boers who came to steal the saddles, etc, of the fallen. He afterwards took part in the advance on Pretoria, and was subsequently present at the surrender of Prinsloo [Brandwater Basin], and later at the action near Bothaville, where Lieut-Col Le Gallais fell. Lieutenant Coulson was granted the DSO for his gallantry in the campaign of 1900."

His DSO award was gazetted on Sep 27, 1901. Earlier, on May 18 at Lambrechtfontein, OFS, he rallied his men and saved the guns, thereby earning the Victoria Cross.

Citation: This officer, during a rearguard action near Lambrechtfontein, on the 18ᵗʰ May, 1901, seeing Corpl Cranmer, 7ᵗʰ Mounted Infantry, dismounted, his horse having been shot, remained behind and took him up on his own horse. He rode a short distance, when the horse was shot, and both Lieut Coulson and the corporal were brought to the ground. Lieut Coulson told Corpl Cranmer to get along with the wounded horse as best he could, and he would look after himself. Corpl Cranmer got on the horse and rode away to the column. No 4792, Corpl Shaw (Lincolns), 7ᵗʰ Mounted Infantry, seeing Lieut Coulson's position of danger, rode back through the rearguard and took him up on his horse. A few minutes later Corpl Shaw was shot through the body, and there is reason to believe that Lieut Coulson was wounded also, as he fell off his horse. Corpl Shaw fell off a few minutes later. This officer on many occasions throughout the campaign displayed great coolness and gallantry under fire. (LG Aug 8, 1902).

According to Sgt Murray Jackson in 'A Soldier's Diary, South Africa 1899-1901' they were near Bothaville: "Young Coulson, our adjutant, rode over and had a look at Tony Welch's grave. They had been very good friends. Poor chap!

He was buried beside Welch within the week..."

After rescuing Cpl Cranmer "... Coulson changed horses with him, and the horse dropping, got left. However, another man went back and got Coulson up behind him; but his horse was shot too, and the man, seeing Coulson lying senseless, thought he was dead (as he may have been), and came away. Coulson's body was found in a mealie patch some paces off, which looks as if he had come round and crawled there for cover." Corporal Shaw was promoted sergeant and awarded the DCM by Lord Kitchener.

Lieutenant Coulson was buried at the scene of the action, on the farm Lambrechtfontein, district Hoopstad. The farm is situated west-south-west of Bothaville.

OD&M: VC, DSO, QSA (Five clasps).

ROGERS, James, 26
Sergeant, South African Constabulary

(Uys)

He was born at Riverina, New South Wales, Australia, on June 2, 1875. Rogers came to South Africa with the First Victorian Contingent. When they returned to Australia in Dec 1900 Corporal Rogers remained and joined the SA Constabulary as a scout. He was promoted sergeant.

According to Wallace, "In June 1901 a column of 500 Royal Irish Rifles were active in the south-east of the Free State, repelling small parties of the enemy who had returned to the area where they had suffered defeat a year earlier. After some skirmishing on the morning of 15 June the column returned in the afternoon to near Thaba Nchu, where a rearguard detachment of two Imperial officers and six men of the South African Constabulary found themselves being attacked by about 60 Boers."

Citation: On the 15th June, 1901, during a skirmish near Thaba 'Nchu, a party of the rear-guard of Captain Sitwell's Column, consisting of Lieut F Dickinson, Sergt. James Rogers, and six men of the South African Constabulary, was suddenly attacked by about sixty Boers. Lieut Dickinson's horse having been shot, that officer was compelled to follow his men on foot. Sergt Rogers, seeing this, rode back, firing as he did so, took Lieut Dickinson up behind him, and carried him for half a mile on his horse. The sergeant then returned to within 400 yards of the enemy, and carried away, one after the other, two men who had lost their horses, after which he caught the horses of two other men, and helped the men to mount. All this was done under a very heavy rifle fire. The Boers were near enough to Sergt Rogers to call upon him to surrender; his only answer was to continue firing. (LG April 18, 1902).

According to Rogers, "I dropped Dickinson behind our rearguard and then prepared to go back for the other two. He shouted, 'You are a fool, you will only get killed,' but I galloped off. I got the other two back all right, and by this time had collected a few bullets through my clothing and hat and had used up all my bullets shooting off my pistol from horseback.

"I later found the Boers to be fine, hospitable people. We beat them only because they fought as individuals and lacked discipline."

The column had stopped behind a high fence beyond a mealie field, half a mile back. Rogers had a bullet through his hat, searing the top of his head, and another through the sole of his boot.

Rogers returned to Australia in Dec 1901, and was commissioned. He then returned to serve with the Cape Police until 1907, then returned to Australia. That year he married Ethel Seldon and they had two sons.

He served at Gallipoli with the ANZACs and was wounded. Captain Rogers served in France before being invalided back to Australia in June 1916 and returned to farming. He lived for many years at Kew, Melbourne, before settling in Sydney. He became Australia's senior VC and is listed in the Australian Dictionary of Biography. He and his wife attended the VC Centenary Ceremony in London in 1956. He died in Sydney on April 28, 1961, aged 85 years. He was given a state funeral at Springvale Cemetery.

OD&M: VC, QSA (Three clasps), KSA (SA01. SA02), 1914-15 Star, BWM, AVM, Coronation Medals 1937 and 1953.

ENGLISH, William John, 18
Lieut, 2nd Scottish Horse, South African Forces

He was born at Cork, Ireland, on October 6, 1882. He joined the 2nd Scottish Horse, a unit raised locally by the Earl of Tullibardine, which served with Col Benson's column in the Eastern Transvaal. Lieutenant English, 18, had recently been promoted when he found himself at Elandshoek (Vlakfontein), near Nelspruit.

(Wilkins)

Citation: William John English, Lieut., 2nd Scottish Horse. This officer, with five men, was holding the right of the position at Vlakfontein, on the 3rd July, 1901, during an attack by the Boers. Two of his men were killed and two wounded, but the position was still held, largely owing to Lieut. English's personal pluck. When the ammunition ran short he went over to the next party and obtained more; to do this he had to cross some fifteen yards of open ground under a heavy fire at a range of from twenty to thirty yards. (LG October 4, 1901).

Three men were killed and nine wounded during the engagement. English's VC was gazetted two days before his 19th birthday. It was awarded to him by the Prince of Wales at the Horse Guard's Parade in London in July 1902, the same time that Clements received his.

After the war English joined the 2nd Dragoon Guards (Queen's Bays) as a lance-corporal. He was commissioned in the ASC in 1906 and posted to Dublin the following year. He commanded a company of the RASC there until Feb 1908, when he was stationed in Cape Town. In 1914 he was promoted captain. He lived at Upper Norwood, Surrey. His wife died in 1918 and in 1922 he married Mary Pyper and had two sons.

In Nov 1924 Major English was stationed in Belfast, Northern Ireland. He transferred to the Indian ASC in 1928, before he retired. During World War II Lieut-Col English commanded a battalion of the Royal Ulster Rifles, then transferred to the Middle East in early 1941. He died aboard a ship in the Mediterranean near Egypt on July 4, 1941, aged 58 years, and is buried in the Maala Military Cemetery, Aden.

OD&M: VC, QSA (Five claps), KSA (SA01, SA02), 1914-15 Star, BWM, AVM, Coronation Medals 1911 and 1937, 1939-45 Star, 1939-45 War Medal, Defence Medal.

CRANDON, Henry George, 27
Private, 18th Hussars (Queen Mary's Own)

He was born at Wells, Somerset, on Feb 12, 1874. Harry Crandon joined the 18th Hussars and in Oct 1894 went to India. He served there until transferred to Natal, where he took part in the Siege of Ladysmith.

After the relief he served with his regiment in various theatres until July 1901, when he and Private Berry were advanced scouts near Ermelo. They came upon a party of Boers and in the fight Berry was wounded in two places and his horse was killed.

(Wilkins)

Citation: On the 4th July, 1901, at Springbok Laagte, Private Berry's horse fell and became disabled, and he was himself shot in the right hand and left shoulder. Private Crandon at once rode back under a heavy fire to his assistance, gave up his horse to the wounded man, to enable him to reach shelter, and followed him on foot, having to run for 1,100 yards, all the time under fire. (LG Oct 18, 1901).

Private Crandon's VC was presented to him by Lord Kitchener at Pretoria on June 8, 1902. He was also promoted corporal. In 1905 Crandon worked at Swinton as a gardener for Sir Lees Knowles. In 1914 he re-enlisted in the 18th Hussars in South Africa for World War I. He was wounded at Ypres in May 1915 then, after his convalescence, sent to the Balkans for two years, then to Egypt and Palestine.

In Nov 1948 Crandon was badly injured in a road accident, sustaining two leg fractures and facial injuries, and spent several months in hospital. His wife, Margaret, died in June 1951. Harry Crandon died at Manchester, Lancashire, on Jan 2, 1953, aged 78 years, and is buried in Swinton Cemetery.

OD&M: VC, India Medal, QSA (Five clasps), 1914-15 Star, BWM, AVM, Coronation Medals 1911 and 1937.

YOUNG, Alexander, 28
Sergeant-Major, Cape Police, South African Forces

(Wilkins)

Sandy Young was born at Ballinona, County Galway, Ireland, on Jan 27, 1873. He joined the Queen's Bays in 1890, where his riding skills brought him to notice. In India he became a Riding Instructor, before seeing active service in the Sudan. Young then joined the Cape Police as an instructor.

In 1897 he performed feats of horsemanship before Queen Victoria, and later before King Edward. He was the champion roughrider of the British army. When the war began his experience of the country and the Boers was extensive. He was to win the VC in a skirmish in Basutoland [now Lesotho].

Citation: Alexander Young, Sergt-Major, Cape Police. Towards the close of the action at Ruiter's Kraal on the 13th August, 1901, Sergt-Major Young, with a handful of men, rushed some kopjes which were being held by Commandant Erasmus and about 20 Boers. On reaching these kopjes, the enemy were seen galloping back to another kopje held by the Boers. Sergt-Major Young then galloped on some 50 yards ahead of his party and closing with the enemy, shot one of them and captured Commandant Erasmus, the latter firing at him three times at point-blank range before being taken prisoner. (LG, November 18, 1901).

He was the only Galway man to win the VC. After the war he went farming near Bulwer in Natal. In 1904 Young served in the Herero Rebellion and was decorated by the Germans, however, when the 1914-18 war began he publicly burnt the decoration. He served in the 1906 Bambata Rebellion, then in the 1914 Rebellion as RSM of the Cape Mounted Police, then in the South West African Campaign.

Young was commissioned in the SA Scottish Bn of the 1st SA Infantry Brigade and served in Egypt and France. He was wounded at the Battle of Delville Wood in July 1916. After his return he was killed at the Butte de Warlencourt on Oct 19, 1916. His name is recorded on the Thiepval Memorial in the Somme and at Bulwer, Natal. Young's medals, excluding the Natal 1906 medal, were sold by Sotheby's in March 1980.

OD&M: VC, Queen's Sudan Medal, Khedive's Sudan Medal, QSA, KSA, Natal 1906 Medal (1906 clasp), 1914-15 Star, BWM, AVM, Coronation Medal 1911.

PRICE-DAVIES, Llewellyn Alberic Emilius, 23, DSO
Lieutenant, The King's Royal Rifle Corps

(Wilkins)

He was born on June 30, 1878, at Chirbury, Shropshire, and educated at Marlborough and Sandhurst. He joined the KRRC in Feb 1898 and in South Africa was wounded three times in the earlier part of the war and mentioned in despatches. In April 1901 Lieut Price-Davies was created a Companion of the Distinguished Service Order.

In September that year he was at the Battle of Blood River Poort, west of Vryheid, Natal, where the Blood River emerges from the Schurweberg. His commander, Gough, impetuously attacked a Boer encampment, only to find some 500 mounted Boers emerge from the Poort. It was the vanguard of Gen Louis Botha's invasion of Natal.

Citation: At Blood River Poort, on the 17th Sept, 1901, when the Boers had overwhelmed the right of the British column, and some four hundred of them were galloping round the flank and rear of the guns, riding up to the drivers (who were trying to get the guns away) and calling upon them to surrender, Lieut Price-Davies, hearing an order to fire upon the charging Boers, at once drew his revolver and dashed in among them, firing at them in a most gallant and desperate attempt to rescue the guns. He was immediately shot and knocked off his horse, but was not mortally wounded, although he had ridden to what seemed to be almost certain death without a moment's hesitation. (LG Nov 29, 1901).

Six officers and 38 men were killed or wounded, while six officers and 235 men were taken prisoners by the Boers.

Price-Davies was promoted captain in Jan 1902. General Kitchener presented him with the VC at Pretoria on June 8, 1902. In 1906 he married Eileen Wilson from Ireland. He served as Adjutant to the 5th Bn Mounted Infantry South Africa until 1907 then, after studying at Camberley, he became Brigade Major, 13th Brigade, Irish Command.

From 1912-14 Price-Davies was GSO3 at the War Office and thereafter of the 2nd and 4th Divisions. He commanded a brigade in France from Dec 1915 to Nov 1917. In Jan 1918 he was created a CMG. From April to Dec 1918 he was employed on special duties in Italy as a major-general.

From 1920-30 he was ADC to the king, 1920-4 Assistant Adjutant General at Aldershot and commanded 145th Infantry Brigade until 1927. He was QMG in

Gibraltar until 1930 and from 1933-48 a Member of the Hon Corps of Gentlemen-at-Arms. During the Second World War he commanded the Upper Thames Patrol (Home Guard). He died at Sonning-on-Thames, Berkshire, on Dec 26, 1965, whereas his wife died in Jan 1973, aged 95 years. His medals are in the Royal Green Jackets Museum at Winchester.

OD&M: VC, CB, CMG, DSO, QSA (Five clasps), KSA (SA01, SA02), 1914-15 Star, BWM, AVM, 1939-45 Star, 1939-45 War Medal, Defence Medal, Coronation Medals 1911, 1937 and 1953.

BRADLEY, Frederick Henry, 23
Driver, 69th Battery, Royal Field Artillery

He was born in London on Sep 27, 1878. Bradley joined the RFA as a Driver and served in the South African War. When General Louis Botha invaded Natal in Sep 1901 he attacked the Itala garrison, south of Vryheid, with 1,600 men.

The British, mainly mounted infantry, held their positions for 19 hours. During the battle Bradley, who would celebrate his 25th birthday the following day, ensured that they would hold on.

(Creagh)

Citation: During the action at Itala, Zululand, on the 26th Sept 1901, Major Chapman called for volunteers to carry ammunition up the hill; to do this a space of about 150 yards, swept by a heavy cross-fire, had to be crossed. Driver Lancashire and Gunner Bull at once came forward and started, but half-way across Driver Lancashire fell wounded; Driver Bradley and Gunner Bull, without a moment's hesitation, ran out and caught Driver Lancashire up, and Gunner Rabb carried him under cover, the ground being swept by bullets the whole time. Driver Bradley then, with the aid of Gunner Boddy, succeeded in getting the ammunition up the hill. (LG Dec 27, 1901).

Driver Bradley was awarded the VC, while Driver Lancashire and Gunners Bull, Rabb and Boddy were each awarded the DCM. Bradley was promoted bombardier and presented with his VC by Lord Kitchener in Pretoria. Bradley remained in South Africa and served in the Zulu Rebellion of 1906 as a mounted machine-gunner in the Transvaal Mounted Rifles.

He was commissioned in the 10th Infantry (Witwatersrand Rifles) and served in South West Africa as OC of C Company. He was attached briefly to the Railway Regiment, before sailing to France to serve in the Royal Field Artillery.

Captain Bradley commanded six batteries of mortars in the Somme until wounded near Delville Wood in Nov 1916. He was then released from the Imperial Army and returned to South Africa, where he joined the Active Citizen Force.

In 1928 Bradley was transferred to the Reserve of Officers with the rank of major. He remained in South Africa and ran a native trading store at one stage. He died in Gwelo, Southern Rhodesia (Zimbabwe) on March 13, 1943. His uniform was on display at the MuseuMAfricA, Johannesburg, whereas his medals were sold by Spinks in Dec 1988.

OD&M: VC, VD, QSA (Talana, Def of Ladysmith, Laings Nek, OFS, Tvl), KSA (SA01, SA02), Natal Medal (1906 clasp), 1914-15 Star, BWM, AVM, Coronation Medal 1937, Colonial Auxiliary Forces LSGC Medal.

BEES, William, 27
Private, 1st Bn, The Derbyshire Regiment

He was born on Sep 12, 1874, at Loughborough, Leicestershire. Bees joined the Derbyshire Regt in March 1890 and served on the Indian Frontier, taking part in the Tirah Campaign of 1897-8. His next active service was in South Africa.

In the Western Transvaal Gen Kekewich's column camped at Moedwil, on the banks of the Selons River, between Rustenburg and Zeerust. On Sep 30, 1901,

(The Register)

they were attacked by Gen De la Rey at 4.45 am. The Boers gained the crest of a nearby hill and fired into the camp. Kekewich was hit twice and the gunners especially suffered severely.

According to the Times History, "A Maxim belonging to the Derbyshires came into action at the south-western corner of the camp, and was served with remarkable devotion. Captains Keller and Baldwin were badly wounded here; and out of a detachment of nine men, six were hit. Private Bees received the Victoria Cross for his gallantry in fetching water from the river under short-range fire from the Boers."

Citation: Private Bees was one of the maxim-gun detachment which, at

Moedwil, on the 30th Sept 1901, had six men hit out of nine. Hearing his wounded comrades asking for water, he went forward, under a heavy fire, to a spruit held by Boers, about 500 yards ahead of the gun, and brought back a kettle full of water. In going and returning he had to pass within 100 yards of some rocks, also held by Boers, and the kettle which he was carrying was hit by several bullets. (LG Dec 17, 1901).

Kekewich repulsed the Boer attack by employing the Scottish Horse in a turning movement. By 6.15 am the fight was over. The British casualties were 214 officers and men while the Boers lost about 60 men.

Bees was promoted corporal on the field of battle. He was discharged in Sep 1902. He married at Loughborough in April 1903, where his best man was Harry Beet VC. His wife, Sarah, and he had a son and a daughter. He rejoined the army in Oct 1914, but was discharged due to illness. From April 1915 he was with the Sherwood Foresters (former Derbyshires) until transferred to the Durham Light Infantry. He served with them in the mining sector for a year and 133 days, then enlisted in the RAMC for the duration. He died at Coalville, Leicestershire, on June 20, 1938, aged 64.

In October 1938 his widow presented his medals to the Sherwood Foresters, as his children had pre-deceased him. His World War I trio were not among the medals.

OD&M: VC, IGS 1895 (Tirah 1897-8), QSA (Three clasps), KSA (SA01, SA02), 1914-15 Star, BWM, AVM, Coronation Medal 1937.

MAYGAR, Leslie Cecil, 29
Lieutenant, 5th Victoria Mounted Rifles, Australian Forces

(Wilkins)

He was born at 'The Dean' Station, Milmore, Victoria, Australia on May 26, 1871. His father's family were originally political refugees from Hungary. He, his father and three brothers owned Strathearn Station, Euroa. Maygar joined the Victoria Mounted Rifles in March 1891 and was commissioned in July 1900. He arrived in Cape Town with the 5th (Mounted Rifles) Contingent in March 1901.

On Nov 23, 1901, the Victorians took part in an engagement at Geelhoutboom in Natal. Lieutenant Maygar went forward to order the retirement of a detachment which were being outflanked. As the troopers retired Trooper A Short had his horse shot under him.

Citation: At Geelhoutboom, on the 23rd Nov 1901, Lieut Maygar galloped out and ordered the men of a detached post, which was being outflanked, to retire. The horse of one of them being shot under him, when the enemy were within 200 yards, Lieut Maygar dismounted and lifted him on to his own horse, which bolted into boggy ground, causing both of them to dismount. On extricating the horse and finding that it could not carry both, Lieut Maygar again put the man on its back, and told him to gallop for cover at once, he himself proceeding on foot. All this took place under a very heavy fire. (LG Feb 11, 1902).

Maygar returned to camp through a gauntlet of fire but was unscathed. Lord Kitchener presented Lieut Maygar with his VC at Pretoria on June 8, 1902. He returned to Australia and continued his commission in the Citizen's Military Force.

On outbreak of the First World War Maygar joined the Australian Imperial Force and served in Egypt and Palestine as a captain with the 4th Australian Light Horse. In June 1917 he was promoted lieut-colonel and received the DSO and Volunteer Decoration. He married Helen Grimshaw of Bristol.

From Oct 1915 Maygar commanded the 8th Light Horse Regiment. During the evacuation of Gallipoli he commanded the rearguard and wrote, "I had my usual luck to be given command of the last party to pull out of the trenches, the post of honour for the 3rd LH Brigade."

LC Maygar, or 'Elsie' as he was affectionately known, was a true fighting commander. He was mortally wounded by an aeroplane bomb at Karm, Palestine, on Oct 31, 1917. His arm was amputated and he appeared to be recovering, then hæmorrhaged and died on Nov 17, aged 46 years. He is buried in the Beersheba War Cemetery and commemorated by a memorial tree at Euroa, Victoria, Australia, a nearby hill named after him and his name in the VC Corner in Canberra, where his medals are displayed.

OD&M: VC, DSO, VD, QSA (four clasps), KSA, 1914-15 Star, BWM, AVM, Coronation Medal 1911.

CREAN, Thomas Joseph, 28
Surgeon-Captain, 1st Imperial Light Horse

The son of a barrister, he was born at Dublin, Ireland, on April 19, 1873. He qualified as a doctor in Dublin, and played rugby nine times for Ireland. In 1896 he came to South Africa as a member of the British Isles rugby team. After the tour he remained behind with his friend, Robert Johnston, a fellow Irishman.

(Uys)

On the outbreak of the South African War they joined the Imperial Light Horse, he as a trooper and Johnston as a captain. Johnston won the VC at Elandslaagte and Crean said to him, "Well, if a b-f like you can win the VC, anyone can!" Crean served through the Defence of Ladysmith and in March 1900 was appointed captain. He gave up squadron command in June 1901 and became a surgeon-captain.

After the abortive third drive to capture De Wet, Gen Dartnell's column returned to Harrismith from Bethlehem, OFS. They were ambushed by De Wet at 11 am at Tygerkloofspruit, 19 miles from Bethlehem. The Boers were repulsed, but heavy firing continued and Crean went to the aid of the wounded.

Citation: During the action with De Wet at Tygerskloof on the 18th Dec, 1901, this officer continued to attend to the wounded in the firing line, under a heavy fire at only 150 yards range, after he had himself been wounded, and only desisted when he was hit a second time, and, as it was first thought, mortally wounded. (LG Feb 11, 1902).

The fighting continued until 2 pm when Dartnell was relieved. That night Dartnell wrote a recommendation for a VC for Crean. Despite his protests Crean was invalided out of the army. The king presented him with the VC at St James's Palace in March 1902. The following year he was awarded the Arnott Memorial Gold Medal as the bravest Irish medical graduate of the war.

In 1905 Crean married Victoria Heredia, of Malaga, and had a son and a daughter. In 1915 he served with the 1st Cavalry Brigade, was twice mentioned in despatches and created a Companion of the DSO (LG June 3, 1915).

In 1916 he commanded the 44th Field Ambulance in France. Major Crean was discharged as medically unfit in Oct 1918. His practice, which had been worth £3,000 a year was broken and by 1922 he was bankrupt. In 1920 he went to money lenders, who charged him £675 interest. The breakdown in his health was the real cause of his financial difficulties.

Crean then served as the medical officer in charge at Ascot, then at various hospitals in Dublin. He died in London on March 25, 1925, aged 51, and is buried in the St Mary's RC Cemetery, Kensal Green, London.

OD&M: VC, DSO, QSA (Elandslaagte, Def of L, Relief of M, Tvl, OFS), KSA (SA01, SA02), 1914-15 Star, BWM, AVM (MID), Coronation Medal 1911, Arnott Gold Medal.

IND, Alfred Ernest, 29
Shoeing Smith, Royal Horse Artillery

(Wilkins)

He was born at Tetbury, Gloucestershire, on Sep 16, 1872. Ind joined the Royal Horse Artillery in Feb 1901 and trained on pom-poms. He was serving in the 11th Section Pom-poms in the OFS when his courage was tested.

General Damant was separated from Rimington, south-east of Frankfort on the Wilge River, when attacked by 300 Boers of the Vrede Commando. The Boers were initially mistaken for Yeomanry until they were close up. In the carnage which followed most of the gunners were shot down around their guns, while Damant was hit in four places.

Citation: During the action near Tafelkop, Orange River Colony, on the 20th Dec 1901, Shoeing-Smith A E Ind, 11th Section Pom-poms, stuck to his gun under a very heavy fire, when the whole of the remainder of the pom-pom team had been shot down, and continued to fire into the advancing Boers till the last possible moment. Captain Jeffcoat, who was mortally wounded on this occasion, requested that Shoeing-Smith Ind's gallant conduct in this, and in every other action since he joined the Pom-pom Section should be brought to notice. (LG Aug 15, 1902).

By the time Rimington arrived to relieve them the British had 33 killed and 45 wounded out of 90 men. Ind was promoted corporal and mentioned in despatches. During further service Ind was wounded and mentioned on another four occasions. His VC was presented to him by King Edward VII at Buckingham Palace in Nov 1901. He served as a lodge keeper to the 2nd Duke of Westminster at Eaton Hall in 1911. Ind died at Eccleston, Cheshire, on Nov 29, 1916, aged 44 years. His VC and medals were sold in 1920 for £105.

OD&M: VC, QSA (OFS), KSA (SA01, SA02), Coronation Medal 1911.

A surgeon at work in the firing line.

1902

MARTIN-LEAKE, Arthur, 27
Surgeon-Captain, SA Constabulary, South African
Forces

(Creagh)

He was born at Standen, near Ware, Hertfordshire on
April 4, 1874. Martin-Leake qualified as a doctor in
London in 1898, then joined the Herts company of the
Imperial Yeomanry and served with them for a year in
South Africa. On their return he remained behind and
was employed by the army as a civil surgeon. When
Baden-Powell formed the SA Constabulary he joined
as a surgeon-captain.

A line of posts held by the SA Constabulary was to be extended to near Van
Tonder's Hoek in the Transvaal. A reconnoitring party of 130 men under Capt
Capell found themselves within 400 yards of a Boer laager, who attacked
them with superior numbers.

On the left centre Sergt Waller was hit in the leg from 40 yards range. Leake
bandaged him then ran to the mortally wounded Lieut Abrahams.

Citation: For great devotion to duty and self-sacrifice at Vlakfontein, 8th
February, 1902, when he went out into the firing line to dress a wounded man
under very heavy fire from about 40 Boers only 100 yards off. When he had
done all he could for him, he went over to a badly wounded officer, and while
trying to place him in a more comfortable position he was shot three times. He
only gave up when thoroughly exhausted, and then he refused water until other
wounded men had been served. (LG May 13, 1902).

The Boers then rushed the position and took the remaining men prisoners.
They expressed regret at having shot Leake, but said that as he rushed from one
side to another they were unaware that he was tending to the wounded. After
being released Leake was recommended for the VC by Gen Baden-Powell.

The VC was presented to Leake by the king at St James's Palace in June 1902.
He qualified as a surgeon the following year then served in India as the medical
officer on the Bengal-Nagpur Railway. In May 1907 his brother, Theodore, a
lieutenant in the Royal Engineers, was drowned off the Dorsetshire coast
following an accident to the war cutter, *Thrasher*.

In 1913 he served with the Montenegran Red Cross. The following year
Lieut Leake was with the RAMC at the First Battle of Ypres, attached to the 5th
Field Ambulance, where he won the first 'double-VC'.

Citation: Clasp to Victoria Cross. Lieut Arthur Martin-Leake, Royal Army Medical Corps (Attached 5th Field Ambulance), who was awarded the Victoria Cross on 13 May, 1902, is granted a clasp for conspicuous bravery in the present campaign.   For most conspicuous bravery and devotion to duty throughout the campaign, especially during the period 29 Oct to 8 Nov 1914, near Zonnebeke, in rescuing, whilst exposed to constant fire, a large number of the wounded who were lying close to the enemy's trenches. (LG February 18, 1915).

The VC bar was presented to Leake by King George V at Windsor Castle in July 1915. Before the war's end Lieut-Col Martin-Leake had commanded a Casualty Clearing Station with the 1st Army. He returned to serve in India after the war. In 1930 he married a widow, Winifred Carroll, but she died two years later.

Martin-Leake had many hobbies, including riding a motorbike and flying his own plane. During World War II he commanded a mobile ARP unit. In his later years he enjoyed fishing, gardening and cooking. Martin-Leake died at Ware, Herts, on June 22, 1953, and was cremated after a service in High Cross Churchyard. His will directed that his medals be given to the RAMC. The author owned his silver cigarette case, with his signature engraved on it. It was lent to the South African Medical Corps Museum, where it was stolen.

OD&M: VC and Bar, QSA (Cape, Tvl, Wittebergen), KSA (SA01, SA02), 1914-15 Star, BWM, AVM (MID), King George V Silver Jubilee Medal, 1939-45 Star, 1939-45 War Medal, Coronation Medals 1937 and 1953, Volunteer Officers Decoration (Indian), Order of Danilo (Montenegro).

The Queen's Scarf

Queen Victoria wished to honour the bravest of the brave in the South African War with a personal token of her regard. She knitted eight scarves, crocheted in khaki-coloured Berlin wool, with the initials 'VRI' on one of the little knots of wool.

Colour-Sergt F Ferret DCM

Mrs Ferret wearing the Queen's Scarf awarded to her husband.

(After Pretoria)

The scarves were to be presented to "the best all-round men taking part in the South African campaign". They were to be allotted to men voted by their comrades as the bravest. Four went to English units and one to each commonwealth country who had sent troops.

Some controversy later arose when it was claimed that the scarves were only issued to men recommended for the Victoria Cross, or that the men had a choice between a VC and the scarf.

There is no evidence to substantiate these claims and it is unlikely that the queen, having instituted the VC as the supreme award for bravery, would then institute another. Lord Roberts mentioned in his despatch of March 1, 1902 that they were gifts from the queen to the most distinguished private soldiers then serving.

"In conclusion his Lordship desires to place on record that in April 1900, her late Majesty Queen Victoria was graciously pleased to send him four woollen scarves worked by herself, for distribution to the four most distinguished private soldiers in the Colonial Forces of Canada, Australia, New Zealand and South Africa, then serving under his command. The selection for these gifts of honour was made by the officers commanding the contingents concerned, it being understood that gallant conduct in the field was to be considered the primary qualification." The four colonial awards were then listed. (LG

16.6.1902).

Queen Victoria had corresponded with her grandson, Prince Christian Victor, who served on General Hildyard's staff during the Relief of Ladysmith. It is likely that he selected the four infantry battalions of the 2nd Brigade, with whom he served. He then joined Lord Roberts as an ADC in Pretoria, where he contracted enteric fever and died on November 29, 1900.

The awards of the scarves to British soldiers were all to sergeants stolid and steady types, whereas the colonial awards were to devil-may-care individuals.

The awards were to:

Imperial:

Britain	Col-Sergt F Ferret DCM	Queen's Royal W Surrey
	Col-Sergt F Kingsley DCM	W Yorkshire Regt
	Col-Sergt H Clay DCM	2nd East Surrey Regt
	Sergt W Colclough	2nd Devonshire Regt

Colonial:

Australia	Private A H Du Frayer	NSW Mounted Infantry
Canada	Private R R Thompson	Royal Canadian Regt
New Zealand	Trooper H D Coutts	NZ Mounted Infantry
South Africa	Trooper L McK Chadwick	Roberts' Horse

BRITAIN

Colour-Sergeant Ferret took part in the Battle of Colenso and was with General Hildyard throughout the campaign. He sent his scarf to his wife in England and it is presently held in the Queen's Regimental Museum.

Frank Kingsley was born in London in 1865, enlisted in 1887 and served for 19 years. He received the QSA with five clasps and the KSA with two clasps. His DCM was awarded for Spion Kop, when he withdrew his men to cover under a heavy cross-fire, then gallantly brought in his mortally-wounded captain.

The Queen's Scarf was presented to Col-Sergt Kingsley at Standerton on August 7, 1900. He was discharged in 1906 and spent his final days as pensioner at the Royal Hospital, Chelsea, where he died on October 26, 1952.

Colour-Sergeant Clay was wounded at Colenso and at Vaalkrantz. His scarf is held by the National Army Museum in Chelsea, London.

Colclough joined the Canadian Army after the war and rose to the rank of lieut-colonel. He died in 1955 and his scarf was deposited in the Manitoba Museum.

AUSTRALIA

(Australian War Memorial)

Du Frayer was recommended for distinguished service on account of bringing in a dismounted comrade under heavy fire on April 11, 1900. Captain Hilliard, commander of C Squadron, NSW Mounted Rifles, reported on an engagement near Karee Siding:

"In April last, when the regiment was on outpost duty near Karee a reconnoitring patrol was sent out in the early morning in charge of Captain Legge. When approaching a farm house flying a white flag, every precaution was taken, but seeing no one about, the men numbering about 12 rode within the stone fence enclosure when they were immediately fired upon from within the house and also by a party of Boers concealed in a donga on the veldt.

"The gateway was only 150 yards from the farm house but Du Frayer dismounted, shook Private Clark into a semi-conscious state and, mounted again, got Clark up behind him and immediately out of danger. Private Du Frayer was exposed to a heavy fire from both quarters previously mentioned."

Du Frayer was commissioned as a 2nd lieutenant, NSW Military Forces. He moved to South Africa and earned the MBE during World War I with the SA Forces. He then moved to Tanganyika [Tanzania] where he died in 1940. His scarf and medals have been presented to the Australian War Memorial in Canberra.

In 1956 his son attempted to have the scarf accredited with a status equal to that of the VC. The Assistant Keeper of the Queen's Archives replied, "... they can hardly be treated as the precise equivalent of the VC. In the first place they were not (so the Stationery Office informs us) gazetted.

"Secondly, they were awarded on a different basis from the VC. One was to go to the bravest soldier in each of the four Colonial contingents fighting in South Africa. To be the bravest soldier in a particular contingent is not, in itself, sufficient qualification for the award of a VC. Clearly then, they must be treated as a separate honour."

CANADA

Richard Thompson was born in Cork, Ireland, in 1867 and emigrated to the United States in 1890. In 1899 he moved to Ottawa where he joined the 43rd Ottawa and Carlton Rifles, then volunteered for service in South Africa with the Royal Canadian Regiment.

According to C Miller the Canadian award to Thompson was for heroism at the Battle of Paardeberg on Feb 27, 1900. "As the dawn was breaking, a captain of a bearer company spotted a wounded man in the field and called for a volunteer to assist him to being the man in. Private Richard Thompson dropped his rifle and ran three hundred yards under fire to his assistance, arriving just before the wounded man was killed by another bullet.

"Although his company commander, Captain Maynard Rogers and Otter recommended Thompson for the Victoria Cross for this and his previous act of heroism, in July 1900 he received one of the seven [sic] Queen's Scarves, knitted by Queen Victoria, for private soldiers in designated units (the Royal Canadians was one of these) after nomination by their commanding officer for most distinguished service in the field."

A similar act of bravery was performed at Paardeberg by Thompson on 18 February. In this case the wounded man bled to death before Thompson could stop the bleeding. Although his gallantry warranted the VC he received the Queen's Scarf. It was shipped to Cork with his personal effects, while he was sent back to Canada, a victim of sunstroke.

Thompson later returned to South Africa and served as a lieutenant in the SA Constabulary, then worked for De Beers in Kimberley. In 1908 he returned to the USA with his Canadian-born wife. On arrival at Buffalo, New York, he died of appendicitis. He was buried with full military honours in Chelsea, Quebec. His scarf was traced in Ireland and is now on display at the National Museum of Canada.

NEW ZEALAND

Henry Donald Coutts was born at Kaiapoi, New Zealand, in 1866. As a young man he moved to Taranaki, where he farmed. From 1881 he served in various volunteer units, then in 1899 went to South Africa with the First Contingent.

At Koorn Spruit he was with the party escorting the guns. "Like several others in the skirmish party, Trooper Henry Coutts was eager to come to grips with the enemy and kept edging forward, worming their way through the long grass until they were well in advance of the guns. This handful of brave but rash men managed to work their way to within 100 yards of the spruit before the Boer fire began to cut them down.

"Finally, accepting that they were attempting the impossible, they started to fall back, but as they did so Coutts noticed a trooper of the Burma Mounted Rifles who had advanced further than any others, lying wounded within 75 yards of the Boer rifles. Coutts hastened his withdrawal until he reached his horse, mounted quickly and dashed forward to pick up the wounded man.

"Many of the Boers stopped firing in their respect for Coutt's mission of mercy, but enough kept blazing away that the New Zealander's act of bravery was most definitely carried out at the peril of his life.

"Remarkably unscathed, Coutts took the wounded man up onto his horse behind him and continued to support him throughout the final dramatic phase of the battle as the mounted contingent moved to outflank the Boers and drive them out of the positions. With the fighting over, Coutts then carried the man the nine miles back to Sanna's Post where the only uncaptured medical section was still operating. Sadly, after all that, the wounded man died just as the post was reached."

It can be said that Koorn Spruit resulted in five VC and two QS awards! Coutts was mentioned in despatches for his bravery. He received his award of the Queen's Scarf at a parade held in Pretoria in September 1900.

He returned to New Zealand in January 1901, where he was presented with a sum of money and a silver mounted sword of honour. Coutts took part in lecture tours, then returned to South Africa as a captain and quartermaster with the 9th Contingent.

He served with the militia until 1910, then in 1913 presented his scarf to the government. It is now housed in the Taranaki Museum. Coutts volunteered for front-line service in World War I, but was refused as he was 48-years-old. He then served in a training battalion in England. He died at Wellington on April 30, 1944, aged 78, presumably still wanting to serve operationally!

SOUTH AFRICA

Leonard McKuiry Chadwick was born at Middletown, Delaware, USA, on Nov 24, 1878. He joined the US Navy and served as an Apprentice, First Class. During the Spanish/American War on May 11, 1898, he was with a boat party attempting to cut a chain in Santiago Harbour under a heavy fire. His courage earned him the Congressional Medal of Honour, the US equivalent of the VC.

Citation: On board the USS *Marblehead* during the operation of cutting the cable leading from Cienfuegos, Cuba, 11 May 1898. Facing the heavy fire of the enemy, Chadwick set an example of extraordinary bravery and coolness throughout this period.

Leonard Chadwick apparently brought mules to South Africa, then decided to join up. A 1902 magazine refers to "a brave American trooper of Roberts Horse who galloped out to save wounded men at Koorn Spruit under heavy fire, and who was later prominent, still under fire, in helping to save the guns."

As reported in 'Black and White Budget' (page 750): "Lord Roberts has confirmed the award of the Queen's Scarf to Trooper Chadwick, of Roberts' Horse, whom his fellow troopers chose as the most distinguished of his corps for bravery. Trooper Chadwick proves to be an American, who was one of the boat's crew who cut the cable across Santiago Harbour during the Spanish American War ... South Africa's scarf has, therefore, gone to America."

In the SA Field Force Casualty List, No 2479 Private L Chadwick is shown as having been taken prisoner by the Boers, together with Privates W Benson and G Redpath. They were captured at Rhenoster on July 28, 1900, and released shortly afterwards.

General De Wet was at Rhenosterpoort, near Schoeman's Drift on the Vaal River. He created a diversion by sending Captain Danie Theron to Rhenoster Kop, 12 miles to the south. On July 28 Theron attacked America Siding unsuccessfully. Presumably he succeeded in taking three unwanted prisoners! [The Times History, Vol IV p 420-1]

Trooper Chadwick proved to be the most decorated of all the Queen's Scarf awardees, for he held the American Congressional Medal of Honour and was awarded the DCM for the Anglo-Boer War. Lord Roberts recommendations for meritorious service of April 2, 1901, refers to J [sic] McKuiry Chadwick, while the DCM award is to J McKinry Chadwick.

Chadwick was next heard of in 1920 at a boarding house in Boston, where he awaited his niece's graduation as a nurse, then accompanied her to Nova Scotia. She later married a Dr Fowler. It is assumed that Chadwick died before 1940.

Although the Queen's Scarf cannot be equated with the Victoria Cross, it served as a personal token of the Queen's gratitude to the bravest men in her forces, and thereby perpetuates the deeds of valour they performed.

Abbreviations

Anzac	Combined Australian & New Zealand troops
ADC	Aide de Camp
AVM	Allied Victory Medal
BWM	British War Medal
Bn	Battalion
CB	Companion of the Bath
CGS	Cape General Service
CMG	Companion of St Michael and St George
CSI	Companion of the Star of India
DCM	Distinguished Conduct Medal
DSO	Distinguished Service Order
Gen	General
GOC	General Officer Commanding
GSM	General Service Medal
GSO	General Staff Officer
Hon	Honourable
IGS	India General Service
KCB	Knight of the Order of the Bath
KCMG	Knight of the Companion of St Michael & St George
KSA	King's South Africa Medal
LG	London Gazette
Lieut	Lieutenant
LSGC	Long Service and Good Conduct
Maj	Major
MID	Mentioned in Despatches
MSM	Meritorious Service Medal
OD&M	Orders, Decorations & Medals
QMG	Quartermaster General
QSA	Queen's South Africa Medal
RAMC	Royal Army Medical Corps
SAGS	South Africa General Service Medal 1877-9
VD	Colonial Auxiliary Forces Officers' Volunteer Decoration

Appendix 1 - MULTIPLE VC AWARDS

Elandslaagte	4	Mullins, Johnston, Meiklejohn, Robertson
Magersfontein	3	Douglas, Shaul, Towse
Colenso	7	Roberts, Congreve, Read, Schofield, Ravenhill, Nurse, Babtie
Mafeking	3	Fitzclarence, Martineau, Ramsden
Ladysmith	5	Digby-Jones, Albrecht, Masterson, Scott, Pitts
Paardeberg	2	Atkinson, Parsons
Koornspruit	5	Phipps-Hornby, Parker, Lodge, Glasock, Maxwell
Wakkerstroom	2	Beet, Nickerson
Krugersdorp	2	Gordon, Younger
Van Wyk's Vlei	2	Hampton, Knight
Geluk	2	Heaton, Brown
Warmbad	2	Bisdee, Wylly
Komati River	3	Cockburn, Turner, Holland
Vlakfontein	2	English, Martin-Leake

Appendix 2 - OTHER VC RECIPIENTS
ASSOCIATED WITH THE ANGLO-BOER WAR

	Theatre	Date of Action
Field Marshal F S Roberts	Indian Mutiny	02.01.1858
General R H Buller	Zulu War	28.03.1879
General G White	Afghanistan	06.10.1879
Col W H Dick-Cunyngham	Afghanistan	13.12.1879
Surgeon-Col E B Hartley	Moirosi Mt	05.06.1879
Lieut-Col R G Scott	Moirosi Mt	08.04.1879
Major R C Nesbitt	Mashonaland	19.06.1896
Lieut the Hon R H de Montmorency	Omdurman	02.09.1898
Major P A Kenna	Omdurman	02.09.1898

Appendix 3 - VCs OF THE ANGLO-BOER WAR
ANALYSED BY REGIMENT

		Posthumous (P)
Australia	5	
Britain	56	6
Canada	4	
India	1	
New Zealand	1	
South Africa	11	1
	78	7

Australia

NSW Medical Corps	1	Howse
Tasmanian Imperial Bushmen	2	Bisdee, Wylly
Victoria Mounted Infantry	1	Maygar
West Australian Mtd Infantry	1	Bell

Britain

Cameron Highlanders	1	Farmer
Derbyshire Regt	2	Beet, Bees
Devonshire Regt	1	Masterson
Dragoon Guards, 5th	1	Norwood
East Surrey Regt	1	Curtis
Essex Regt	1	Parsons
Gordon Highlanders	6	Meiklejohn, Robertson, Towse, Mackay, Gordon, Younger (P)
Highland Light Infantry	2	Shaul, Kennedy
Hussars, 10th	2	Milbank, Engleheart
14th	1	Brown
18th	1	Crandon
Imperial Yeomanry, 3rd	1	Doxat
King's Liverpool Regt	3	Hampton, Knight, Heaton
King's Own Scottish Borderers	1	Coulson (P)
King's Royal Rifle Corps	2	Roberts (P), Price-Davies
Lancers, 5th	1	Dugdale
17th	1	Lawrence
Manchester Regt	2	Scott, Pitt
RAMC	4	Douglas, Babtie, Inkson, Nickerson

Rifle Brigade	2	Congreve, Durrant
Royal Berkshires	1	House
Royal Engineers	2	Digby-Jones (P), Kirby
Royal Field Artillery	3	Nurse, Reed, Bradley
Royal Horse Artillery	7	Schofield, Nurse, Phipps-Hornby, Parker, Lodge, Glasock, Ind
Royal Irish Regt	1	Barry (P)
Royal Scots Fusiliers	1	Ravenhill
West Riding Regt	1	Firth
West Yorkshire Regt	2	Mansel-Jones, Traynor
Yorkshire Light Infantry	1	Ward
Yorkshire Regt	1	Atkinson (P)

Canada

Royal Canadian Dragoons	3	Cockburn, Turner, Holland
Strathcona's Horse	1	Richardson

India

Indian Staff Corps	1	Maxwell

New Zealand

4th New Zealand Contingent	1	Hardham

South Africa

Cape Police	1	Young
Imperial Light Horse	4	Mullins, Johnston, Albrecht (P), Crean
Protectorate Regt	2	Martineau, Ramsden
Rimington's Guides	1	Clements
SA Constabulary	2	Rogers, Martin-Leake
Scottish Horse	1	English

Appendix 4
VC's OF THE ANGLO-BOER WAR IN ORDER OF GAZETTING

London Gazette 1900

Feb 3	Congreve, Roberts, Nurse, Reed,
Apr 20	Babtie, Phipps-Hornby, Parker, Lodge, Glasock
July 6	Towse, Fitzclarence, Milbanke, Martineau, Ramsden
July 20	Meiklejohn, Norwood, Robertson
July 27	Mansel-Jones
Aug 10	Mackay
Sep 14	Richardson
Sep 28	Gordon, Ward, Shaul, Younger (memo)
Oct 5	Engleheart, Kirby
Nov 13	Bisdee
Nov 20	Parsons
Nov 23	Wylly

London Gazette 1901

Jan 1	Halliday
Jan 4	Knight
Jan 15	Brown, Inkson, Doxat, Lawrence, Curtis
Jan 18	Heaton
Feb 12	Nickerson, Beet, Mullins, Johnston
March 8	Maxwell
March 29	Douglas
April 12	Farmer
April 19	Digby-Jones (memo), Albrecht (memo)
April 23	Cockburn, Turner, Holland
June 4	Howse, Masterson, Clements, Ravenhill, Firth
July 26	Scott, Pitts
Aug 30	Schofield
Sep 17	Dugdale, Traynor
Oct 4	Bell, English, Hardham
Oct 18	Hampton, Crandon, Kennedy, Durrant
Nov 8	Young
Nov 29	Price-Davies
Dec 17	Bees
Dec 27	Bradley

London Gazette 1902

Feb 11	Crean, Maygar

Apr 18	Rogers
May 13	Martin-Leake
Aug 8	Younger, Digby-Jones, Albrecht, Coulson, Atkinson, Barry
Aug 15	Ind
Oct 7	House

Appendix 5 - **INVESTITURES**

March 4, 1900 by General Buller at Ladysmith: Nurse, Reed.

July 18, 1900 by Queen Victoria at Windsor: Towse.

August 20, 1900 by Queen Victoria at Osborne: Robertson.

October 25, 1900 by Lord Roberts at Pretoria: Babtie, Congreve, Phipps-Hornby, Fitzclarence, Mackay, Lodge, Norwood.

October 28, 1900 by Lord Roberts at Pretoria: Ramsden.

December 15, 1900 by Queen Victoria at Windsor: Milbanke, Meiklejohn, Engleheart, Glasock, Ward.

July 25, 1901 by King Edward VII at St James Palace: Wylly, Mullins. Johnston.

August 14, 1901 by the Duke of Cornwall & York at Pietermaritzburg: Maxwell, Curtis, Farmer, Ravenhill, Shaul, Heaton, Brown.

August 19, 1901 by the Duke of Cornwall & York at Cape Town: Kirby.

October 11, 1901 by the Duke of Cornwall & York at Toronto: Cockburn.

October 14, 1901 by the Duke of Cornwall & York at Quebec City: Turner.

November 1901 by King Edward VII at Buckingham Palace: Ind.

December 17, 1901 by King Edward VII at St James Palace: Kennedy, Doxat.

March 2, 1902 by King Edward VII at St James Palace: Crean.

General Buller presenting VCs to Capt Reed and Cpl Nurse at Ladysmith in March 1900.

June 2, 1902 by King Edward VII at St James Palace: Martin-Leake.

June 8, 1902 by Lord Kitchener: Price-Davies, Maygar, Crandon, Bradley, Pitts, Scott, Knight.

July 1, 1902 by the Prince of Wales in London: Hardham, Bell, English and Clements.

July 2, 1902 by Col C S Browne VC at York: Traynor.

August 1902 by King Edward VII in London: Lawrence.

September 18, 1902 by Lord Tennyson at Melbourne, Australia: Rogers.

October 2, 1902 by King Edward VII at Buckingham Palace: Dugdale.

July 1915 by King George V at Windsor: Bar to VC to Martin-Leake.

Appendix 6
ANGLO-BOER WAR VCs KILLED DURING WORLD WAR 1

Fitzclarence	11.11.1914	1st Ypres, France
Martineau	08.04.1916	Died at Dunedin, NZ
Maxwell	21.09.1917	Ypres, France
Maygar	31.10.1917	Palestine
Milbanke	21.08.1915	Dardanelles
Norwood	08.09.1914	Sablonnieres, France
Young	19.10.1916	Butte de Warlencourt, Somme, France

Appendix 7 - CEMETERIES IN WHICH INTERRED, OR PLACES DIED/COMMEMORATED

	Cemetery/Town	Deceased	Age at Death
Aden	Maala Military Cem	English	58
Australia	Melton Mowbray, Tas	Bisdee	60
	Sydney	Rogers	85
Belgium	Knocke	Babtie	61
	Menin Gate	Fitzclarence	49
Canada	Quebec, Mt Hermon Cem	Turner	89
	Ontario (Ashes)	Holland	70
	Rupert, Vancouver	Beet	72
	Toronto, St James Cem	Cockburn	45
Dardanelles	Gallipoli	Milbank	42
England	Barnet, Herts	Curtis	74
	Birmingham	Ravenhill	49
	Blackburn, Lanc	Pitts	77
	Blandford, Dorset	Knight	77
	Bristol	Bell	79
	Brockenhurst, Hamps	Mansel-Jones	70
	Brompton, London	Farmer J	76
	Brookwood, Woking, Surrey	Meiklejohn	42
	Camberley, Surrey	Wylly	81
	Cambridge	Doxat	75
	Chichester, Sussex	Inkson	74
	Coalville, Leic	Bees	64
	Coventry, Warwickshire	Parker	48
	Datchet, Berks	Engleheart	65
	Droitwich, Worc	Douglas	63
	Dover, Kent, St James Cem	House	32
	Dover, Charlton Cem	Traynor	85
	Eccleston, Cheshire	Ind	44
	Goring-on-Thames, Berks	Towse	84
	Liverpool, Lanc	Nurse	72
	Liverpool, Lanc	Farmer D	88
	Liverpool, St James Cem	Richardson	60
	London	Brown	78
	London	Lodge	57
	London	Gordon	74
	London	Howse	66

Country	Place	Name	
	London	Reed	61
	London	Schofield	66
	London, Kensal Green	Crean	49
	London, Richmond	Hampton	49
	London, Tottenham	Durrant	68
	Longborough, Glos	Dugdale	24
	Manchester, Lanc	Crandon	78
	Sheffield, York	Firth	47
	Shorncliffe, Kent	Doogan	86
	Sidcup, Kent	Kirby	84
	Sonning, Berks	Phipps-Hornby	89
	Sonning, Berks	Price-Davies	87
	Southport, Lanc	Heaton	66
	Thirsk, Yorkshire	Hill	84
	Tring, Herts	Osborne	70
	Ware, Herts	Martin-Leake	79
	Waterlooville, Hamps	Masterson	73
France	Nice	Mackay	56
	Sablonnieres	Norwood	38
	Thiepval Memorial	Young	43
	Ypres Reservoir Cem	Maxwell	46
Ireland	Downpatrick, Co Down	Scott	86
	Dublin	Murray	83
	Kilkenny	Johnston	77
	Limerick	Danaher	58
Israel	Beersheba War Cem	Maygar	45
Kenya	Nakuru	Lawrence	75
Malta	At sea	Congreve	54
New Zealand	Dunedin	Martineau	42
	Wellington	Hardham	62
Scotland	Edinburgh	Robertson	84
	Edinburgh, Merchiston	Kennedy	31
	Cour, Kintyre	Nickerson	79
South Africa	Belfast	Barry	27
	Boksburg	Shaul	80
	Chieveley Station	Roberts	27
	Maitland, Cape Town	Glasock	36
	Cape Town (Ashes)	Ramsden	57
	Jacobsdal district	Parsons	24
	Grahamstown	Mullins	46
	Krugersdorp	Younger	29

118

	Ladysmith	Digby Jones	23
	Ladysmith	Albrecht	23
	Hoopstad district	Coulson	22
	Newcastle	Clements	64
	Paardeberg	Atkinson	26
Wales	Glamorganshire	Ward	44
Zimbabwe	Gwelo	Bradley	66

Bibliography

Abbott, P E, and Tamplin, J M A, *British Gallantry Awards* (1971) Guinness Superlatives Ltd, London.

Amery, L S, *The Times History of the War in South Africa* (1907) Sampson Low, Marston & Co Ltd, London.

Arms & Armour Press, *South African War Honours and Awards*, 1899-1902 (1971) in association with Hayward & Hall.

Boyder, Doug, Correspondence regarding the Queen's Scarf.

Creagh, Sir O'Moore, & Humphris, E M, *A Complete Record of the VC and DSO* (1924) Standard Art Book Company.

Dooner, Mildred, *The Last Post* (1980), J B Hayward & Son, London.

Hall, Major D, *The Hall Handbook of the Anglo-Boer War 1899-1902* (1999) University of Natal Press, Pietermaritzburg.

Imperial War Museum, *The Victoria Cross and George Cross* (1971).

Lehmann, Joseph, *The First Boer War* (1972) Military Book Society.

Lummis MC, Canon William. His research papers at the National Army Museum at Chelsea, London.

Mikula M, *The Adams Story* (1981) Durban.

Miller, C, *Painting the Map Red* (1993) Canadian War Museum.

Moorhead, Murray J, *The Queen's Scarf,* an appraisal of one of the most bewildering and controversial British military awards of all time (1978) Unpublished article.

Orford, Julian, Article on *The Queen's Scarf* in *Home Front* and letter from Henk Loots.

Smyth, Sir John, VC MC Bt, *The Story of the Victoria Cross 1856-1963* (1963) Muller, London.

The Register of the Victoria Cross (1981), This England.

The Victoria Crosses and George Crosses of the Honourable East India Company & Indian Army 1856-1945 (1962) National Army Museum.

Timmermans, Owen, *Reading History with the Metal Detector*, in Treasure Talk, Durbanville, First Quarter 2000.

Toomey, T E, Heroes of the Victoria Cross (1895), Newnes, London.

Uys, Ian S, *The History of Southern Africa's Victoria Cross Heroes* (1973) Uys Publishers, Cape Town.

Uys, Ian S, *Delville Wood* (1983) Uys Publishers, Germiston.

Wallace, R L, *The Australians at the Boer War* (1976) The Australian War Memorial and the Australian Government Publishing Service, Canberra.

Wilkins, Philip A, *The History of the Victoria Cross* (1970) Benchmark Publishing Co Inc, New York. Originally published in 1904.

Wilson, H W, *With the Flag to Pretoria* (1900) Harmsworth Bros Ltd, London.

Wilson, H W, *After Pretoria: The Guerrilla War* (1902) Harmsworth Bros Ltd, London.

Wulfsohn, Lionel, *Rustenburg at War* (1987) L M Wulfsohn, Rustenburg.

www The Internet Various Victoria Cross References.

Index

Lancashire Regt, See King's Own	
Lawrence B T T	64
Lodge I	49-50
Lord Strathcona's Horse	58
Mackay J F	4-5
Mafeking	8-9 12 26-9
Magersfontein	17-9 59
Majuba	3 6-7
Manchester Regt	37 66
Mansel-Jones C	43-4
Martineau H R	26-7
Martin-Leake A	101-2
Masterson J E I	35-6
Matabele Rebellion	26
Maxwell F A	51-2
Maygar L C	96-7
Meiklejohn M F M	9-11
Milbanke J P	30-2
Moedwil	95-6
Montenegro	101
Mosilikatse Nek	63
Mullins C H	12-3
Murray J (1881)	1-2
Naauwpoort	82
New Zealand	82 104 106
Nickerson W H S	53
Nooitgedacht	79
Northampton Regt, See Regt 58th	
Norwood J	14-5
Nottinghamshire Yeomanry	30
Nourse's Horse	2
NSW Medical Corps	61
Nurse G E	25
Olympic Games	64
Osborne J (1881)	5
Paardeberg	38-9 87 106
Parker C E H	49
Parsons F N	38-9
Phipps-Hornby E J	46-50
Pitts J	37-8
Price-Davies L A E	93-4